CHIEFS SPECIAL DIAMOND JUBILEE

SMITH & WESSON

Chiefs Special

DIAMOND JUBILEE
1950–2025

Fine Nib Publishing
Atlantic City, Wyoming

Bob Townsend

Fine Nib Publishing
Copyright © 2025 by Bob Townsend
All rights reserved. No part of this book may be used or reproduced
in any manner whatsoever without written permission.

First Edition

Printed in the United States of America

The terms and logos AIRWEIGHT, LADY SMITH, BODYGUARD,
SMITH & WESSON, M&P, PERFORMANCE CENTER, S&W, and
CHIEFS SPECIAL are registered trademarks of Smith & Wesson, Inc.
Smith & Wesson reserves all rights, title, and interest to their trademarks
provided herein. Used by permission.

The term DymondWood is a registered trademark of Rutland Plywood,
Rutland, Vermont. Rutland Plywood reserves all rights, title, and interest
to their trademark, and it is used herein by permission.

The Lyman and Merrie Wood Museum of Springfield History, in
Springfield, Massachusetts, owns the rights to images of items in its
collections. Figure 2 and its inset on page 12 are two of those items.
Used herein by paid Image Usage Agreement with the museum.

Universal/NBC obtained the rights for the two **DRAGNET** movie
posters, Figures 61 and 62, on pages 50 and 51. Used herein by paid
license agreement with Universal/NBC.

Images are either the author's or are accredited.

ISBN: 979-8-9929682-3-1 (hardcover)
ISBN: 979-8-9929682-2-4 (paperbound)
ISBN: 979-8-9929682-4-8 (e-book)
Library of Congress Control Number: 2025913351

Cover design by Barbara Townsend
Front cover: Chiefs Special serial number 38185.
Back cover: Chiefs Special serial number 38174.
Smith & Wesson shipped them to its Los Angeles
sales representative in June 1954, and he presented
them to the stars of the 1950s **DRAGNET** radio
and television programs and the 1954 movie.

to

Dr. Roy G. Jinks

Mentor and Friend
Smith & Wesson Historian

No free man shall ever be debarred the use of arms.
—Thomas Jefferson

Contents

Smith & Wesson Historian Dr. Roy G. Jinks transformed my interest in Chiefs Specials into a passion. He supplied the mountains of information I analyzed to conduct this review: from envisioning the small Model J revolver through production, naming it the Chiefs Special, its frequent alterations, and subsequently other models and model numbers spawned through these seventy-five years. "Thank you" pales compared to the dedication Dr. Jinks contributed to my collection of details. Most consequentially, though, he became a friend and constant correspondent along this path. I extend my most heartfelt thank you, Roy.

Jean Jinks deserves my special thanks. Many a time Jean served as a courier to mail all sorts of stuff Roy believed I should have to help me reach this goal. Jean, you're a delightful lady, and I enjoyed meeting you at the annual Smith & Wesson Collectors Association symposium in 2023 in Glendale, Arizona. Jean, I thank you most sincerely for your wonderful support through the years.

I thank these other two score and two Smith & Wesson friends who enabled my learning and my Chiefs collection: Robert Wayne Bass, Larry Bennett, Mike Bliss, Thom Braxton, Jim Brewster, Guy Bruner, David Carroll, Jim Carter, Joe Cebull, Charlie Clark, Jim Craig, Dr. Bill Cross, Jim DeMarco, Jeff Donnell, Jim Fisher, Charles Flick, Danny Fowler, Richard Garner, Les Goggess, Tom Graham, Gil Granado, Tom Harney, John Heckert, Tom Horwedel, Lee Jarrett, Ryan Keevan, Russ Lindenlaub, Brian McGilvray, Don Mundell, Rick Nahas, Jack Phelps, Bob Radaker, Al Rettke, Ray Richards, Tom Schubert, Rich Sopko, Mike Speers, Alan Tong, Robert Vivas, Kevin Williams, John Witty, and Francis Zandome. These friends shared finds to bolster my database, provided scads of the seemingly minor details I gobbled up, sold guns and other bits to me, and continuously challenged me by asking tough questions. I most heartily thank each and every one of you.

Two organizations and their members became strong allies in my quest: The Smith & Wesson Collectors Association and the Smith & Wesson Historical Foundation. Chairman Dr. Bill Cross took the initiative to send archived documents and provide other details I didn't even know to ask for. Thank you, Dr. Cross, and all.

Thanks, too, to Lee Jarrett for his *Smith & Wesson Forum* and its terrific members. Their worldwide willingness to share is ever special. You'll hear from folks whose inputs proved essential to help me narrate the Chiefs' story. Thank you, Lee, and all.

On a different level I thank *Police Chief* Magazine Editor Danielle Gudakunst and her team for researching and sharing Smith & Wesson's advertisements from past issues and the annual conference dates of her magazine's parent: The International Association of Chiefs of Police. Dani's information provided previously unknown details and helped me weave new threads into a tapestry covering far more than a hypothesis of early events. I doff my hat and thank you, Dani.

Three Springfield, Massachusetts, folks proved invaluable: Curator of History Elizabeth Kapp and Assistant Registrar Stephen Sullivan, at the Lyman and Merrie Wood Museum of Springfield History, and Museum Collections Curator Alex MacKenzie at the Springfield Armory National Historic Site. These two sites house the first, second, and third Chiefs Specials to leave Smith & Wesson's Roosevelt Street plant in Springfield. Serial number **6** is Wood Museum Object ID WMSH-98.01009, and serial numbers **X58** and **10** are Springfield Armory catalog numbers SPAR 2248 and 2249. A thousand thanks to Elizabeth, Stephen, and Alex for their time, answering my myriad questions, and supplying and arranging for photos I've included in Chapter 1.

For reviewing the book and especially for suggesting which of my Chiefs to put on the cover, I thank my pal Jim *"Howya Doon?"* DeMarco.

You wouldn't be reading this if not for my friend and publisher, Barbara Townsend. Her keen eye and commitment to making this better than I could have envisioned was inspirational. Barbara flipped every rock as she harnessed artistic, grammatic, style, and technical details, including legal and professional permissions, licensing, trademarks, and the other million elements that must be attended to. Barbara has mastered the process.

Another friend, marketing savant Julie Adelmann, shared her deft skills. Barbara's artistic genius harnessed Julie's font layout ideas to craft a cover and wrap the bundle in a professional and attractive cloak. Their collaborate efforts far surpassed anything my creative deficit could have conjured up. I offer up my most sincere admiration, appreciation, and a million thanks, Barbara and Julie.

Smith & Wesson produced one revolver for the United States and our allies' needs during World War II. Postwar S&W reintroduced popular prewar models and expanded offerings with new models. This study portrays the evolution of one of those new models in its Diamond (seventy-fifth) Anniversary year: the first J-frame, the Chiefs Special.

I won't ask you to navigate a tedious litany of academic citations from the pen of Smith & Wesson Historian Dr. Roy G. Jinks: *History of Smith & Wesson*, pages 224-233; Smith & Wesson Collectors Association *Journal* article from the Fall 2005 issue, pages 51-54, where he offered ship dates and the dispositions of the first seventy-five Chiefs; historic letters; and several forms of personal communication.

Many moons ago Dr. Jinks rescued up to 300,000 pages of S&W history from landfill fate. He is *the* primary source of production numbers and the production sequence; engineering changes; invoices; shipping dates, documents, and destinations; model introductory dates; advertisements; internal memos; experimental notebook pages; engineering design records; and more. Things came to me via phone conversations, mail, and email. Most dates are lost to long-gone calendars, but the facts live on.

Analysis-based opinions come from observation as I built my collection and gathered details for a database of more than 20,000 Chiefs. Invoices and serial number lists add more examples than I have seen. I report serial numbers of first and last known models and features I have seen in person, in photos, or from friends' inputs. Data analysis comes from a far deeper place than an admirer's casual glance. I ogle plain-Janes along with the exotic models; each told its story, and I listened. I lean toward pragmatism—facts, not fantasy—so I tend not to speculate about things I don't know. I ask questions. I trust you will ponder alternatives and then come up with your own interpretations. None of us will ever *know it all.*

I set out to build a Chiefs Special collection that would stand alone to tell the model's story. Early on I wondered, "How many Chiefs will it take?" I believed the number would be small. Silly me. Especially through the model's first decade refinements and modifications came at a fevered pace. When I felt confident I'd learned enough, I began to narrate the story of the model's first fifty years in articles for the Smith

& Wesson Collectors Association *Journal*. After the editor accepted an installment and before it went to press new information came into view, altering small bits of the story. Such is the nature of documenting history. Here I offer a consolidated and much revised view of those six articles. The story could change before you get the book in hand.

Revised features overlap in serial and shipping order. No neat, logical flow exists. I offer first and last known features in serial number order. The next formerly unknown Chiefs Special to show up after being hidden in someone's sock drawer for a half-century could rewrite history.

Smith & Wesson neither produced nor shipped revolvers in serial number order. With few exceptions I feature the Chiefs in ship date order. We rarely get to know which day the company assembled, completed, or readied a revolver for shipping; however, we can find out which day Smith & Wesson shipped most of them. Others taught me to consider a gun's birthday the day S&W shipped it. The rule generally makes good sense, but you'll see instances where guns shipped long after what many would consider their serial number's production year.

Historic events I correlate to three shipping dates in the story came from a speech I offered at a United States Air Force gala during the September 1999 Constitution Week celebration at Kirtland Air Force Base, New Mexico. I was thrilled when I discovered three Chiefs in my collection shipped on those dates. Several of my life's personal events and fond memories match or are near other ship dates.

What's in a name? You'll see how the model got its plural name. Chiefs Special is protected by trademark. You'll see how S&W employees misused the original, official name, calling it a singular Chief Special or a possessive Chief's Special. Novices and collectors still do the same.

Through time folks have adopted nicknames S&W never used. I lean toward purist thinking and try to use terms the company assigned. In many cases the company did not use a modifier to distinguish parts, some attributes, or even models. The lack of an official descriptive or distinguishing name might explain why folks come up with creative adjectives. In a few instances I find value in folks' descriptive terms and use them with special appreciation (e.g., "contoured" or "flat" thumbpiece). In general, though, too many modifiers add fluff but describe nothing.

Some—nay, many—paint early five-screw Chiefs Specials with the nickname "Baby Chiefs." I admit to having been snared by the trap early on. I believe the term relates to the small, round trigger guard and short grip frame, and I've outgrown it. For context I've not heard anyone call a Terrier with a five-screw frame a Baby Terrier, and it began life smaller and far earlier than the Chiefs Special. It's a five- or four- or three-screw Chiefs Special, and later it's a Chiefs Special plus a model number.

The contrived "Model of 1953" moniker seems to portray one iconic S&W four-screw I-frame—"1953 .22/32 Kit Gun"—as identified in 1953 and later catalogs. Painting a J-frame with the broad-brushed name misinterprets the facts. Smith & Wesson neither introduced nor made a major modification to any J-frame model in 1953. The company did not use the year to identify any Chiefs Special model. Having developed then shipped its first-full production four-screw Chiefs Special Airweights in fall 1952, S&W completely bypassed 1953 and replaced its carbon steel five-screw Chiefs Special with a four-screw model in late spring 1954.

My lexicon does not include the modifiers "no-dash," "pre-lock," or "pre-model." Users of the first term seem to imply a model without a "dash number" is superior; you'll see that's pure fallacy regarding Chiefs ranging from the mid-1960s into the late 1980s. S&W named each of its revolvers and later added model numbers so it was a Chiefs Special then it added Model 36. Other terms are noise—like static on a radio.

Another pair of adjectives some use in conjunction with far too many models include "rare" and "scarce." Like profanity, you won't find them in my writings. Marketing and sales folks who seem to have ties to P. T. Barnum dilute the truly unique marques by using the terms in nearly every auction or sale listing. Pshaw!

A last bit of grit I need to pick from my craw relates to those supposed informed folks who go on ad nauseum about the earliest Chiefs Specials being built on a modified I-frame. Balderdash! The ridiculous claim is akin to saying S&W built L- and X-frame revolvers on a modified K-frame. S&W adapted another frame's traits (i.e., trigger guard and grip frame size). K-, L-, and X-frame stocks interchange, as do I- and J-frame stocks on models with the same number of frame screws. Simple as that!

Enough carfuffle. *Off we go …*

I have carried a revolver; lots of us do, but they are the most innocent things in the world.
—Mark Twain

Guns are normal and normal people use guns.
—David Yamane

Part 1

Revolvers

The Constitution shall never be construed to
prevent the people of the United States
who are peaceable citizens from
keeping their own arms.
-— Samuel Adams

Chapter 1

1950

Model J five-screw
.38 Chiefs Special five-screw

Near the Great Depression's end and under the leadership of Smith & Wesson President Harold Wesson, the company introduced its 2" barreled .38/32 Terrier—a 32 I-frame round butt revolver chambered for an impotent .38 S&W cartridge. Slightly larger in diameter but stumpy, the .38 S&W cannot stand up to the highly respected .38 S&W Special, a cartridge reportedly too long for a tiny I-frame's short cylinder window.

Harold Wesson passed away after World War II, and for the first time in its ninety-plus-year history the company hired as its president a gentleman who did not have the Wesson family name.

In 1949 Smith & Wesson President Carl R. Hellstrom levied a challenge on the company's engineering department: Build a small-frame revolver that will fire .38 S&W Special cartridges.

Perhaps learned revolver devotees will excuse my simpleminded digression; I will inject it nonetheless. The revolver Hellstrom envisioned would function in double action, pulling the trigger through in one smooth motion to both cock and fire the revolver, and in single action, manually cocking the hammer to lock it in place, then pulling the trigger to fire it.

The International Association of Chiefs of Police (IACP) met in Colorado Springs, Colorado, the next year, October 7-12, 1950, for its fifty-seventh consecutive annual conference.[1] S&W sent its marketing team, and they asked the assemblage of chiefs to submit fitting names for a new five-shot revolver chambered in .38 S&W Special.

Dr. Roy Jinks said that on Monday, October 23, 1950—eleven days after the chiefs' conference concluded—President Hellstrom told Smith & Wesson's manufacturing department to deliver a J-frame revolver chambered in .38 S&W Special to him in his office and to charge it on a memorandum account.

According to Dr. Jinks' review of company production records, S&W completed the first three J38 revolvers the next day. Dr. Jinks told me, "Serial number **6** and two others were 'probably completed' that day." Manufacturing created and sent a memo to shipping. Shipping recorded the memorandum and delivered Model J serial number **6** to President Hellstrom on Friday.

According to the S&W invoice, "MODEL J BLUE Ser. #6," was "Delivered to Mr. C.R. Hellstrom, President Smith & Wesson, Inc., Springfield, Mass.," on October 27, 1950 (Figure 1).

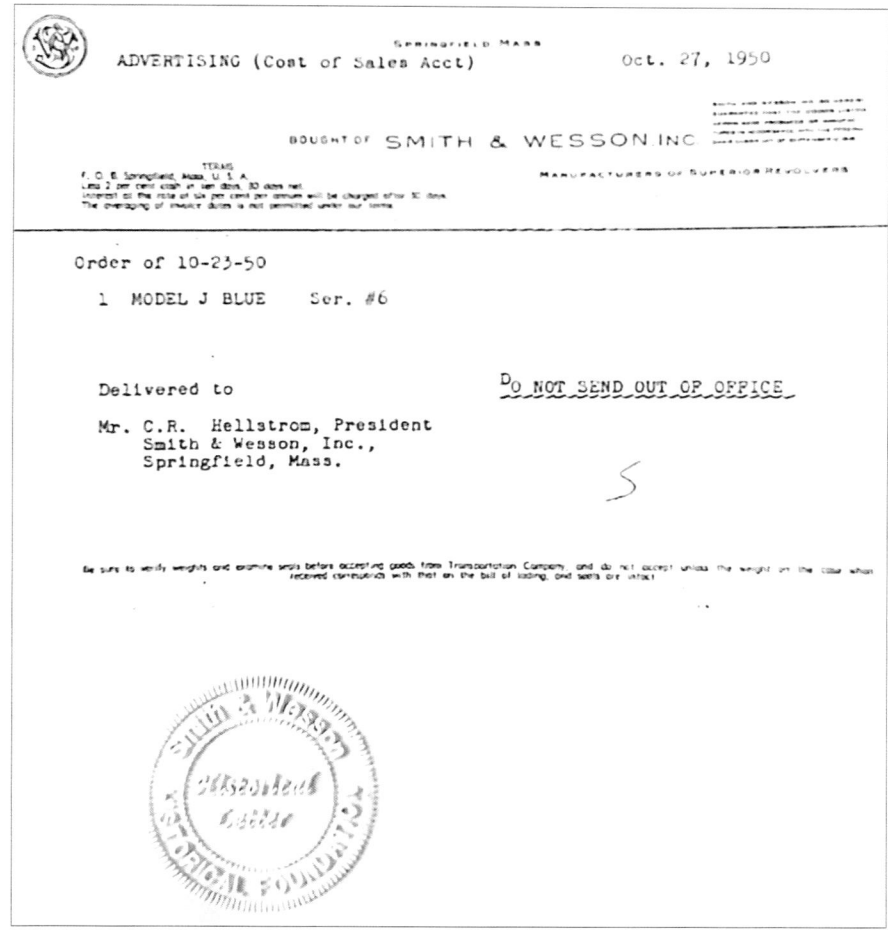

Figure 1: The first Model J invoice. (Courtesy of Dr. Bill Cross)

Dr. Jinks told me Advertising or Memorandum invoices with <u>DO NOT SEND OUT OF OFFICE</u> text printed on them only went to the accounting department for tax purposes.

By chance I discovered Model J serial number **6** is housed in the Lyman and Merrie Wood Museum of Springfield History, in Springfield, Massachusetts.[2] The museum's Curator of History Elizabeth Kapp told me the museum acquired President Hellstrom's Chiefs Special in 1998 "as a part of the larger donation of materials from Smith & Wesson."

The Lyman and Merrie Wood Museum of Springfield History Assistant Registrar Stephen Sullivan arranged the agreement for me to obtain professional photographs of serial number **6**, which the museum identifies as "*.38 Model J Chiefs Special* by Smith & Wesson [98.01009]" (Figure 2). The serial number on the butt has two dots stamped beneath it, perhaps to avoid confusing serial number **6** with serial number **9** (inset). Serial number **6** wears the first known contoured thumbpiece and serial number-matching checked walnut round butt diamond magna stocks with S&W medallions and diamonds surrounding flush-mounted screw and nut escutcheons, a service type front sight, and a square notch rear sight. The caliber on the right side of the barrel reads 38 S. & W. SPL.

Figure 2 & inset: Smith & Wesson delivered its first Model J, serial number **6**, to S&W President Carl Hellstrom. "*.38 Model J Chiefs Special* by Smith & Wesson [98.01009]" is serial number **6**, and it currently resides in the Wood Museum of Springfield History, in Springfield, Massachusetts. (Photography by John Polak) (Per Image Usage Agreement with the Lyman and Merrie Wood Museum of Springfield History, Springfield, Massachusetts. Gift of Smith & Wesson.)

Smith & Wesson's advertisement in IACP's December 1950 *Police Chief* Magazine includes President Hellstrom's letter to Police Chief Edward Boyko of Passaic, New Jersey (Figure 3). The first two paragraphs of President Hellstrom's November 15, 1950, letter said:

> We have unanimously selected the name "Chiefs Special" for our new revolver, and I want to congratulate you on being the first to submit this name on ballot #45 at the Police Chiefs' Convention.

Since this revolver was especially designed for police work, the name "Chiefs Special" seems most appropriate. Your name is now being engraved on the prize gun, and we will forward it to you within a few days.

Figure 3: S&W's ad in *Police Chief*, December 1950. (Courtesy of IACP/*Police Chief*)

The invoice for bright blue Model J serial number **29** says S&W engraved *Chief Edward Boyko* on the gun and shipped it to him in Passaic, New Jersey, on December 15, 1950. It wears diamond service stocks and the same new contoured thumbpiece as serial number **6**.

The revolver shown in the Smith & Wesson ad is not a Model J. I suggest it is one-of-a-kind "I 38 Special" serial number **X54**. A partial page from S&W's experimental notebook describes **X54** with a shortened .38 S&W Special cylinder stuffed into an I-frame's tiny cylinder window (Figure 4). The I-frame's $1\frac{7}{8}$" barrel pokes into its cylinder window so **X54**'s longer .38 Special cylinder required the shorter $1\frac{3}{4}$" barrel. An I-frame's extractor and rod have right hand threads. I cropped the bottom of the page, which documents a test shooter put 2,045 .38 Special rounds through **X54** in June 1950. S&W's sales team did not have a Model J to show to the chiefs in early October. Did the team show **X54** to the chiefs?

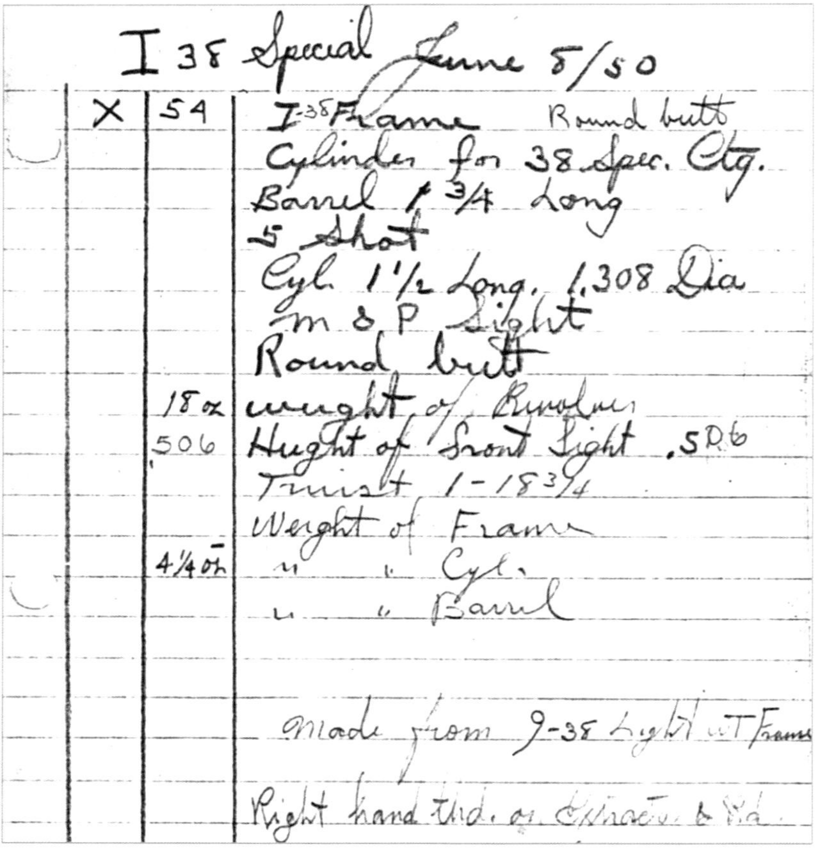
I 38 Special June 8/50
X 54 I-38 Frame Round butt
Cylinder for 38 Spec. Ctg.
Barrel 1 3/4 Long
5 Shot
Cyl. 1 1/2 Long. 1.308 Dia
M & P Sight
Round butt
18 oz weight of Revolver
.506 Height of Front Sight .506
Twist 1-18 3/4
Weight of Frame
4 1/4 oz " " Cyl.
" " Barrel
Made from I-38 Light Wt Frame
Right hand thd. on Extractor & Rod

Figure 4: S&W's **X54** experimental notebook page. (Courtesy of Dr. Roy Jinks)

Model J's stretched frame accommodates its 1.53" long cylinder, according to Dr. Jinks' review of S&W's engineering design records. The round butt J-frame adopted the I-frame's round trigger guard and short exterior grip frame dimensions, but inside the beefed-up Model J grip frame a coil mainspring replaced the I-frame's flat mainspring (Figure 5).

Figure 5: *Left:* Model J coil mainspring. *Right:* I-frame Terrier mainspring and strain screw.

A ball atop the rod inside Model J's mainspring nests in a socket in the base of the hammer (Figures 6 & 7).

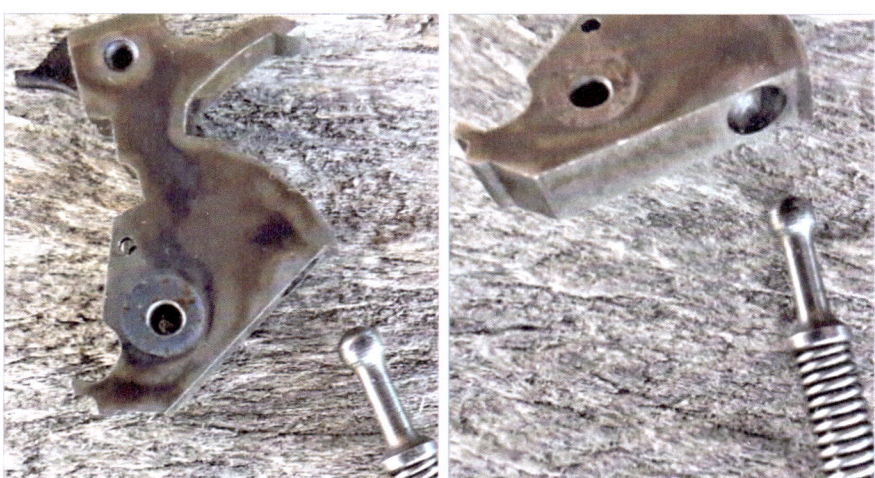

Figures 6 & 7: Model J mainspring rod's ball and socket arrangement.

S&W used the I-frame photo it used in the *Police Chief* ad in other Chiefs Special ads (Figure 8). The domed head of the I-frame's mainspring strain screw stands proud on the front strap. President Hellstrom's serial number **6** has the Model J's coil mainspring so it does not have the strain screw. Prices show $60 for blue and $66 for nickel.

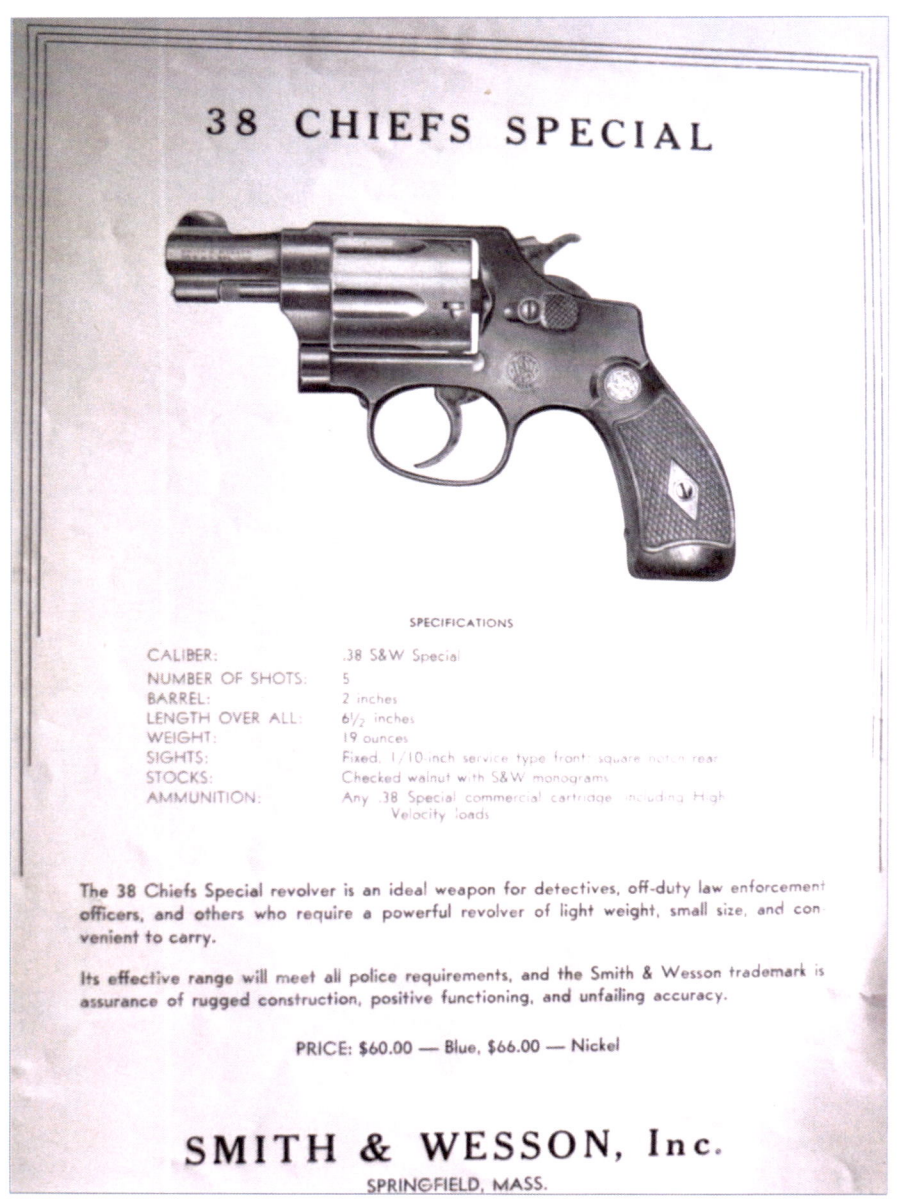

Figure 8: Early, undated S&W Chiefs Special flyer. (Courtesy of Dr. Roy Jinks)

Its barrel stampings and thumbpiece highlight two more disparities between the revolver pictured in Smith & Wesson's advertisements and the Model J. The caliber stamped on the left side of the barrel below the company name—the standard location for an I-frame Terrier—reads .38 S&W SPL. CTG.; however, the caliber stamped on known Model Js and Chiefs Specials is on the barrel's right side, and it does not include the abbreviation for cartridge. The era-standard I-frame thumbpiece, like the one shown in the ad, has an hourglass waist between its nut and the contour where the thumb fits. Early Model Js use either new full-bodied contoured thumbpieces sans an hourglass waist, like the one on serial number **6**, or a new flat thumbpiece.

Smith & Wesson's new five-screw J-frame revolvers have four screws on the side plate and one ahead of the trigger guard. The Model J weighs 19 ounces, and it is 6½" long with a nominal 2" barrel (measure is 1⅞"). Model J's extractor and rod have left hand threads. Did S&W employ this feature because the right hand threads on **X54**'s extractor and rod unthreaded when the test shooter fired the more powerful round?

Dr. Jinks told me production records show S&W completed 112 Model Js in 1950, including ten with 3" barrels between December 6 and 16 and two with nickel finishes on December 22. After delivering Model J serial number **6** to President Hellstrom in October S&W shipped the next eighteen Model Js in December. Serial numbers ranged from **8** to **X59**.

Richard Nahas, coauthor with Jim Supica of *Standard Catalog of Smith & Wesson, Editions 1-5*, sent several Chiefs photos to me in July 2025. A photo taken at Springfield Armory in March 1993 shows the left side of serial number **10** wearing the second known set of round butt diamond magna stocks and the first flat thumbpiece. On December 6, 1950, Model J serial numbers **X58** and **10** went to S&W's Assistant Sales Manager Walter Sanborn so he could deliver them to the Springfield Armory. Richard's photo inspired me to contact the Springfield Armory National Historic Site (NHS) to find out if serial numbers **X58** and **10** are still there.[3]

The curator sent photos of the two to me. One photo shows serial number **10** stamped inside the right walnut magna stock. We now know it's one of the first three Model Js to leave the factory with magna stocks (Figure 9). It is also one of the first two Model Js to leave with the new flat thumbpiece, and it's an oddity among the string of flat thumbpieces that evolved through the next fifteen years.

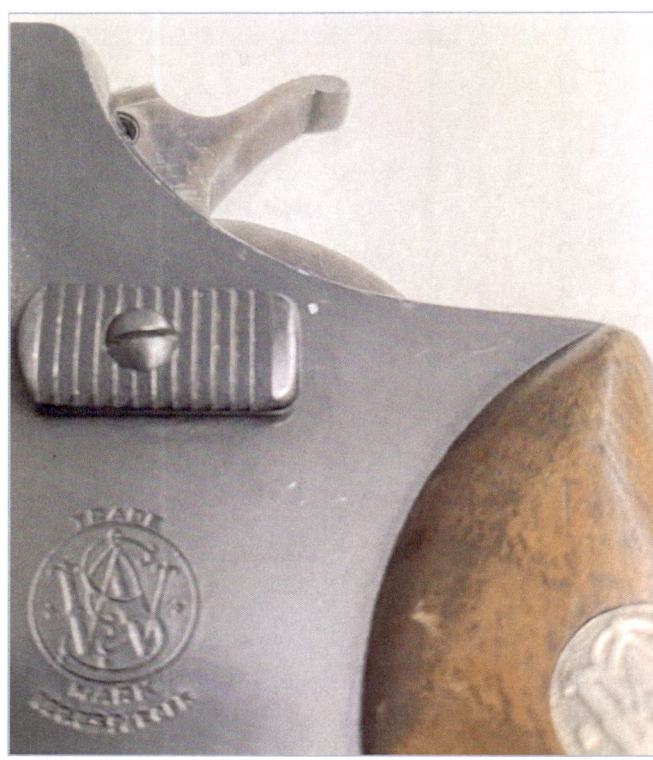

It is an anomaly due to the fact it only stands ¼" tall, offers a svelte look, and has squared edges on the bottom, top, and right. Other known Chiefs with this flat thumbpiece include serial numbers **X58**, **16, 32, 54, 99,** and **101**.

Figure 9: Model J serial number **10**. (Courtesy of the Springfield Armory NHS)

Another pair of the curator's photos show the butt and left side of serial number **X58**, the first square butt Model J. Finding it roughly parallels the monumental discovery of the whereabouts of Model J serial number **6**. My database lists four known carbon steel five-screw square butt Chiefs Specials in the first 46,000 serial numbers.

Figure 10 shows the serial number on the butt of **X58**. S&W assigned the X to its experimental models, and as a general rule they typically followed different paths than standard production models.

Figure 10: The square butt of serial number **X58**. (Courtesy of the Springfield Armory NHS)

Serial number **X58** wears the first flat thumbpiece, serial number-matching square butt diamond magna stocks, and a 2" barrel (Figure 11).

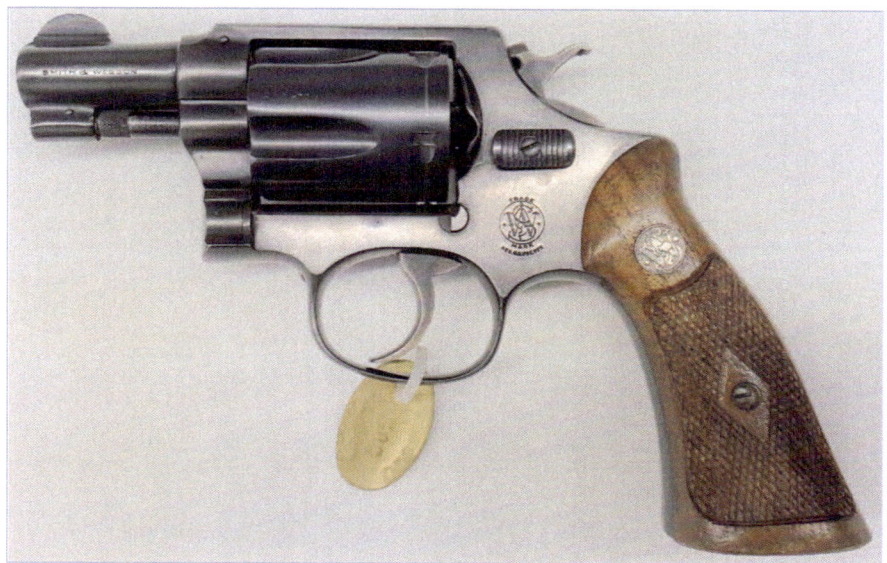

Figure 11: Square butt serial number **X58**. (Courtesy of the Springfield Armory NHS)

Smith & Wesson Collectors Association friend Tom Schubert sent this invoice to me (Figure 12). It features a 3" barrel on square butt, blue, serial number **X58** when Mr. Sanborn delivered it to Springfield Armory.

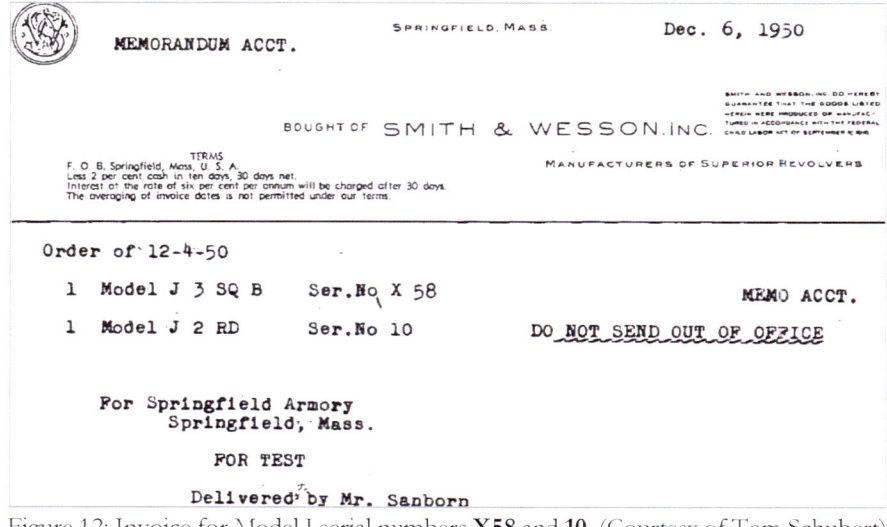

Figure 12: Invoice for Model J serial numbers **X58** and **10**. (Courtesy of Tom Schubert)

Dr. Jinks sent Smith & Wesson's November 1950 experimental notebook page for serial number **X58** to me (Figure 13). It lists barrel lengths 3¾", 2½", and 3", but it doesn't list the 2" barrel, which bears serial number **X58**, now on the revolver. Like the invoice, it mentions the square butt frame. The photo of the revolver made me wonder if the grip frame on the square butt is significantly longer than the round butt.

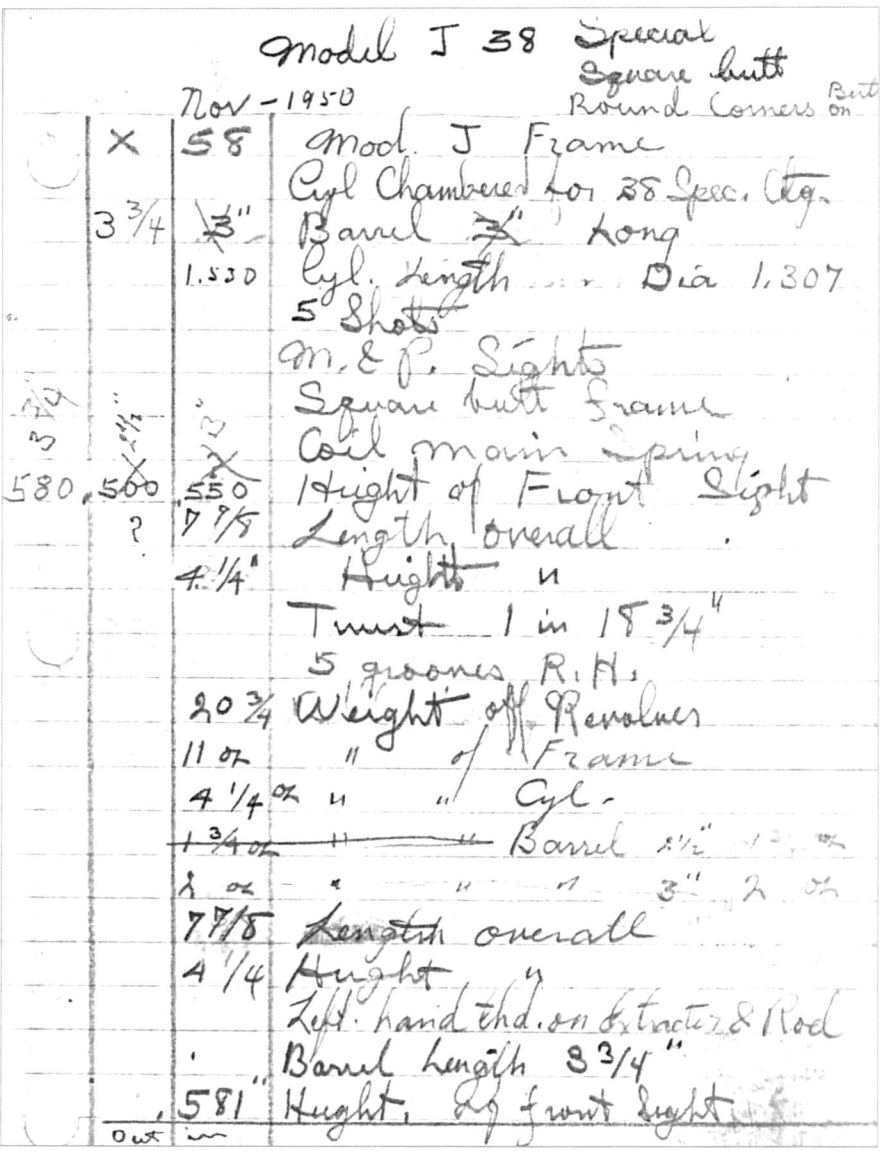

Figure 13: S&W's notebook page for serial number **X58**. (Courtesy of Dr. Roy Jinks)

The curator's new photo confirms the J-frame square butt has a longer grip frame (Figure 14). Postwar "square butt" I-frames had round butt grip frames with a relieved back strap for a special square butt stock.

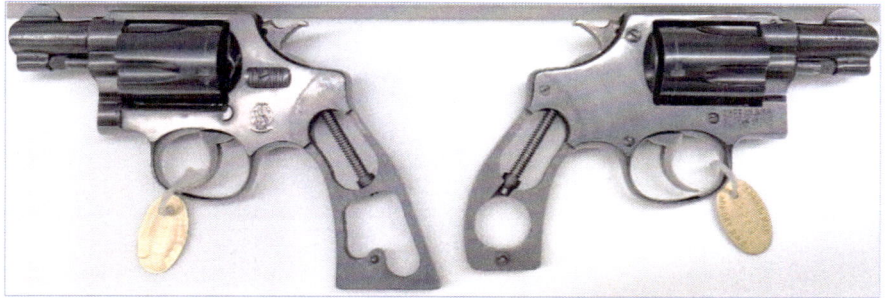

Figure 14: *Left*: Square butt serial number **X58**. *Right*: Round butt serial number **10**. (Courtesy of the Springfield Armory National Historic Site)

Dr. Jinks' Smith & Wesson Collectors Association *Journal* article in 2005 said the armory returned serial number **10** to S&W on June 28, 1951. The article doesn't say the same about **X58**. The curator told me the two weren't "put in the museum until May 21, 1965," so he cannot account for their whereabouts until then, but he said it was an "internal transfer" so it's clear S&W had returned serial number **10** to the armory.

Serial numbers **X59**, 3" barrel and the second with a square butt, and **40**, 2½" barrel, went to Walter Sanborn on December 15, 1950.

Tom Schubert owns serial number **19**. It has a bright blue finish and is engraved *John M. Olin*. S&W shipped it on December 18, 1950, to John Olin, president of Olin Industries. Tom also owns serial number **21**. It's engraved *A. M. Johnson*. S&W shipped it to Lieutenant Colonel A. M. Johnson on December 18, 1950, in Georgetown, Washington, D.C.

Other than serial numbers **X58** and **10**, most other known early Model Js wear the contoured thumbpiece. Serial number **32** shipped on December 26, 1950, to New York City Police Lieutenant Robert Pardua. It has the flat thumbpiece. S&W engraved *Robert Pardua* on its bright blue finish, and it wears smooth rosewood presentation stocks. Characteristic of presentation stocks, S&W stamped a two-digit number, not the gun's serial number, on the inside of both stocks. Another Smith & Wesson Collectors Association friend owns serial number **32**.

- -

Wouldn't I like to find one of the Model Js shipped in 1950?

Dress suitably in short skirts and sitting boots,
leave your jewels and gold wands in the bank,
and buy a revolver.
—Constance Markievicz

Chapter 2

1951-1954

.38 Chiefs Special
>   Carbon steel five-screw
>   Aluminum alloy Airweight five-screw
>   Aluminum alloy Airweight four-screw

Dr. Jinks told me Smith & Wesson produced 1,740 Chiefs Specials in 1951, and as near as I can reckon that year's shipments totaled about 1,600. The first, serial number **9**, went to the Chilean Naval Mission in Washington, D.C., on January 6, 1951, and the last known serial number, **1825**, went to Wesson Farms in Victoria, Arkansas, on November 26, 1951.

S&W applied a satin blue finish on most Chiefs Specials and put a special bright blue finish on some gifts. Smith & Wesson's January 30, 1951, invoice for eight revolvers lists five "Chief Special": three bright blue serial numbers **2**, **30**, and **43**, and two nickel serial numbers **3** and **7**. A note on the invoice says, "Gift guns for Venezuela per Mr. Hellstrom's directions." S&W engraved the five Chiefs Specials to Venezuelan civilian and military officials.

S&W engraved names of Brazilian members of the Joint Brazil-United States Military Commission on eleven 3" Chiefs Specials serial numbered **23** to **52** and then shipped them to Colonel Antonio Bastos in Washington, D.C., on March 7, 1951.

S&W created Chiefs Special serial number **72** with its bright blue finish as a gift for Flora (Mitchell) Van Orden (Figure 15). It is engraved and wears a small hammer and a smooth trigger (Figure 16 & insets). Other early features include a $\frac{1}{10}$" wide service type front sight, square notch rear sight, barrel pin, and small S&W logo on the left side of the frame below the new contoured thumbpiece. The serial number-matching checked walnut service stocks bear S&W medallions and diamonds that surround flush-mounted screw and nut escutcheons.

Short service stocks allow the rear side plate screw to be domed so it matches the other side plate screws. Taller presentation and diamond magna stocks require the rear side plate screw to have a flat head.

Flora Van Orden's daughter, also named Flora, posted a thread on the *Smith & Wesson Forum* saying her mother and S&W President Carl Hellstrom were friends. The invoice for Flora's revolver identifies it as a "Chief Special J-38." S&W shipped it on March 7, 1951. The caliber stamped on the right side of the barrel reads 38 S. & W. SPL., and the four lines of text stamped on the lower right side of the frame note Made in U.S.A., trademark registration, and company name and location.

Figure 15: The features on Flora Van Orden's gift conjure up a charming *je ne se quoi*.

Figure 16: *F.M. VAN ORDEN*. Insets: *Top*: Small hammer. *Bottom*: smooth trigger.

Flora Van Orden and her husband George Van Orden owned the Evaluators Limited Gun Shop. Figure 17 shows a black-and-white photo I received with her Chiefs Special (photographer unknown). The Van Ordens are to the right of Flora's Chiefs Special. A caption written on the back of the photo identifies Philip Roettinger to the left. He and General Van Orden served in the United States Marine Corps during World War II. After the war Roettinger became an operations officer at Central Intelligence Agency, which is near the Van Orden's gun shop in Quantico, Virginia.

Figure 17: *Left* to *Right*: Philip Roettinger, Flora and George Van Orden.

This condensed summary offers a look at the standard Chiefs Special production sequence. A worker fits and then stamps a random assembly number on three parts: on the frame in the yoke cut, on the yoke, and inside the side plate (Figures 18-20).

Figures 18-20: *Left* to *Right*: A random assembly number stamped on the frame in the yoke cut, on the yoke, and inside the side plate.

The frame goes to a stock fitter who stamps serial numbers on the butt and inside the right stock (Figures 21 and 22). This is the only time during the production process frames are in serial number order.

Figure 21: *Left*: Serial numbers stamped inside the right stock and on the butt.
Figure 22: *Right*: This is a good one to show how to read a Chiefs Special's butt serial number. Point the barrel left, and rotate the butt up to read its serial number.

The "soft fitter" fits the barrel, the yoke, and the cylinder with its extractor onto the frame; disassembles the revolver; and stamps serial numbers on those four parts (Figures 23-26). Next he sends the parts to their polishing and finishing stations. The "hard fitter" reunites the parts, completes a final assembly, and applies his mark. Then sans stocks the revolver goes to the range for a proof test—the standard tests consist of firing live ammunition through three cylinders, but the tester fires live ammunition through all cylinders on one in ten guns. If the revolver passes the proof test, the tester stamps a tiny dot in the rear lower corner of the cylinder window ahead of the frame lug. Following another inspection the Chiefs Special goes back to the stock fitter. Then it's off for one final inspection, packaging, and shipping, or it goes into the vault. (Per a phone conversation with Dr. Jinks with fine tuning and clarifications via email.)

Figures 23-26: *Left* to *Right*: Serial numbers stamped on the bottom of the barrel, back of the yoke, back of the cylinder, and the inside face of the extractor.

Smith & Wesson's earliest known use of aluminum to produce a Chiefs Special came with the experimental notebook entry for "Model JA 38 Special" serial number **X65** on February 24, 1951 (Figure 27).

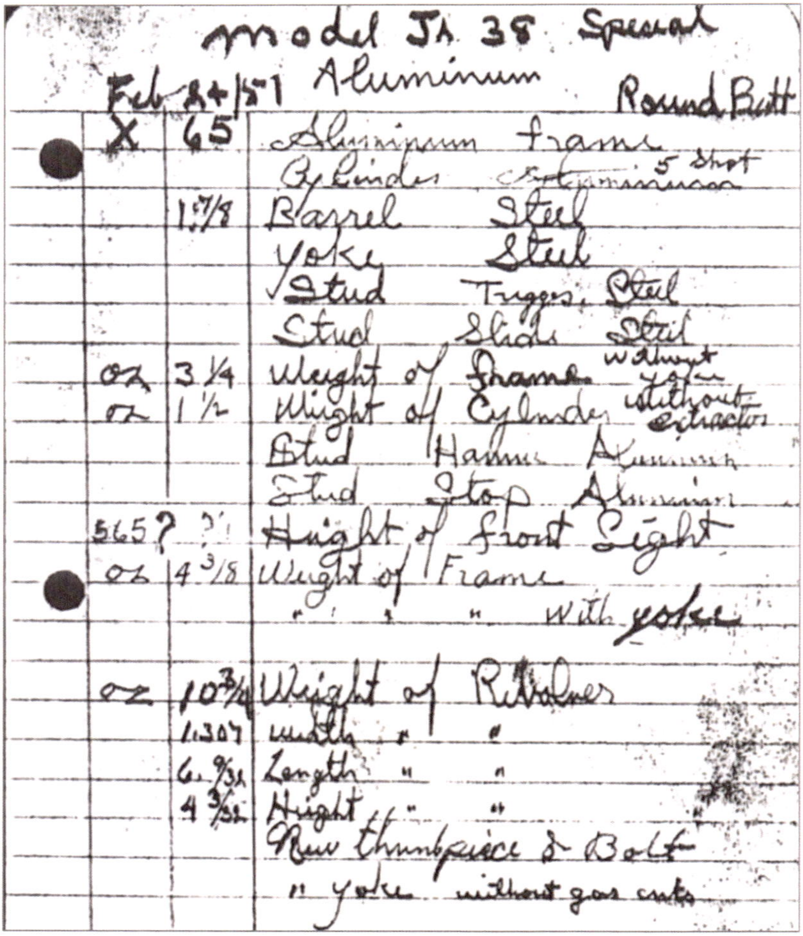

Figure 27: S&W's experimental notebook page for serial number **X65**. (Courtesy of Richard Nahas)

Richard Nahas offered a terrific presentation on the Smith & Wesson aluminum Airweight revolvers on June 13, 2025, at the annual Smith & Wesson Collectors Association symposium in Concord, North Carolina. He passed around serial number **X65** through a room of more than 100 of us in attendance with the special request: "I'd like to get the gun back after my presentation." He did. This is the first known Chiefs Special Airweight built on the five-screw frame. Richard explained this Airweight traveled to Germany early in its lifetime and while there was engraved with an oak motif and then gold washed. The owner replaced its original round butt diamond magna stocks with these round-to-square-butt conversion stocks, also engraved with an oak motif (Figure 28). The experimental notebook identified the unusual thumbpiece as the "New Thumbpiece & Bolt," suggesting perhaps a contoured thumbpiece and its special bolt had been replaced (inset). Surprisingly, the thumbpiece is serial numbered **X65** on the back side, a thing I hadn't seen before. Other points of interest include no "Airweight" stamp anywhere on the gun, and an agreeable gold filigree adorns the hammer and trigger. I had asked the symposium event coordinator and official photographer Rex Halfpenny to shoot images of Richard's gun to use here. Richard let us borrow his Airweight unsupervised for a scant few minutes. Thanks to you both.

Figure 28: From S&W's experimental notebook: serial number **X65**. Inset: The "New Thumbpiece." (Courtesy of Richard Nahas and Rex Halfpenny)

"Chief Special" serial number **111** shipped on April 11, 1951, to Naval Air Station Corpus Christi, Texas. The invoice said, "Hold for Attache Express" for Rex Applegate. It has the first known second flat thumbpiece, a ³⁄₈" tall oval, and it wears diamond magna stocks. At some point Lieutenant Colonel Applegate returned it to S&W to be engraved. The next known Chiefs Specials with this thumbpiece are my plain-Jane serial number **261** and Tom Schubert's serial number **337**, which S&W President Hellstrom delivered to Federal Bureau of Investigation Director J. Edgar Hoover in his office in Washington, D.C., on October 29, 1951.

Richard Nahas entertained us for an hour with his tales of the Airweight revolvers. He included a discussion of the Aircrewman models; Jim Supica and he thoroughly cover the topic in their book so I do not. Richard also showed us Chiefs Special Airweight serial number **A13933**, built on a Chiefs Special five-screw aluminum frame (Figure 29). He let me borrow it, too, so Rex could shoot the images of it.

Figure 29 & inset: Chiefs Special Airweight serial number **A13933**. Future Airweight serial numbers do not have an A prefix. (Courtesy of Richard Nahas and Rex Halfpenny)

While **A13933** was probably produced later than the other serial numbers identified near here, it may be the last Airweight made on the five-screw frame. It includes the word Airweight stamped on the right side of the barrel above the 38 SPECIAL CTG caliber stamp (inset).

Richard later told me, "That gun never left the factory until the Smith & Wesson factory collection went to auction in 1996 at Butterfields in CA." It wears the second flat thumbpiece and diamond magna stocks.

Chiefs invoices offer sparse details about each revolver: barrel length, finish, and sometimes butt—round or square. If it doesn't identify presentation stocks, the invoice doesn't say whether the standard walnut stocks are service or magna. Unless the gun has a specifiable feature a Chiefs Special invoice does not mention the number of frame screws, front sight, hammer, trigger, thumbpiece, or other details. We must see each revolver to know its configuration. Interpreting database information presents a challenge; S&W made millions of Chiefs, and I've documented far fewer than one percent in each serial range. It's a fruitless endeavor to guess at the configuration of the next unknown serial number.

The fifth known nickel Chiefs Special, serial number **84**, wears a contoured thumbpiece and diamond service stocks. The next known factory nickel Chiefs come in an order for fifteen in the 1300-1500 serial range. S&W shipped serial number **84** to John Beckmann in Mineola, Nassau County (Long Island), New York, on May 24, 1951. The county executive had appointed Beckmann as county police commissioner in October 1945, according to Smith & Wesson Collectors Association friend Francis Zandome, who had read the online newspaper account.

On May 24, 1951, S&W also sent satin blue Chiefs Special serial number **117** to John Beckmann. It wears the last known diamond service stocks and contoured thumbpiece. The Smith & Wesson shipment to Beckmann contained twenty-five Chiefs Specials, the largest shipment of early Chiefs, and twenty-four were blue. The serial numbers ran from **67** through **118** and included several strings of consecutive serial numbers.

Serial number **54** wears serial number-matching diamond magna stocks, and it shipped with serial numbers **61** and **76** on June 19, 1951.

Both early flat thumbpieces have eleven ridges and twelve valleys. Serial numbers **10**, **16**, **32**, **54**, **X58**, **99** (Figure 30), and **101** wear the only known examples of the first flat, ¼" tall thumbpiece (inset). Future flat thumbpieces are ⅜" tall. S&W shipped serial number **99** on August 20, 1951, to Charles Greenblatt Company in New York City. It wears a satin blue finish and matching-serial number diamond magna stocks, which remained the standard on Chiefs for more than fourteen years.

Figure 30: Chiefs Special serial number **99** wears serial number-matching diamond magna stocks. Inset: ¼" tall first flat thumbpiece.

Two friends own serial numbers **16** and **101**. S&W shipped the pair on August 24, 1951, to W.A. Harvey Sporting Goods in Syracuse, New York, for the Reception Center at the Department of Corrections in Elmira, New York. The invoice identifies them as "Chief Special." Serial number **16** wears diamond magna stocks, but the right stock has no serial number, suggesting the original stocks had been replaced. Serial number **101** wears matching-serial number diamond service stocks.

Tom Schubert owns serial number **16**, and he also owns Chiefs Special serial number **54**, which I have mentioned before. It was one of three designated for New York City Police Department officers, and Smith & Wesson shipped it to Charles Greenblatt Company in New York City on June 19, 1951. Another one I have mentioned before found its way into my collection this year. Smith & Wesson shipped serial number **261** on October 17, 1951, to E. K. Tyron Company in Philadelphia, Pennsylvania (Figure 31). The shipment included five Chiefs Specials in serial range 259-301. Both of these Chiefs—serial numbers **54** and **261**—have a smooth trigger. My **261** wears a second flat thumbpiece, but except for it neither Tom nor I have seen Chiefs Specials between serial numbers **117** and his **337** so we do not know which thumbpieces any of the Chiefs Specials within that serial range wear.

Figure 31: Chiefs Special serial number **261** wears a smooth trigger.

S&W's September 14, 1951, engineering change #313 for Model I and J triggers said, "Add serrations to front." The first known J-frame with a serrated trigger is serial number **631**, shipped to J. L. Galef & Son Incorporated in New York City on December 3, 1951. The last known serial numbers with smooth triggers are **4875**, shipped on June 6, 1952, and an outlier, **8338**, shipped on May 15, 1952.

My calculations suggest S&W shipped upward of 21,000 Chiefs Specials in 1952. The range of known carbon steel Chiefs Special serial numbers shipped in 1952 begins at **132** and ends at **24825**.

Smith & Wesson blocked 901 serial numbers in range 2773-3673 for a Japanese order for 780 Chiefs. S&W shipped the order to Japan in January 1952, and known invoices show the company shipped 105 of the 901 in the Japanese serial block to distributors in the United States.

S&W shipped serial number **3729** in February 1952. It and serial number **11661**, owned by a Smith & Wesson Collectors Association friend, have the last known service type front sights. S&W shipped **11661** to Charles Greenblatt Company in New York City on April 28, 1952.

Engineering change #312, August 31, 1951, for "Ramp Sight" for I and J 1⅞" barrels said, "Change to straight taper. Eliminate Margin and Radius." A note on a September 4, 1951, invoice for serial number

224 said, "New Ramp Sight." It went to S&W Superintendent Bill Gunn. On January 10, 1952, engineering change #323 for I and J barrels said, "Add .010 to sight heights." We see the first confirmed $\frac{1}{10}$" wide smooth ramp front sight on serial number **2928** (Figure 32 and inset). It wears the second flat thumbpiece and is one of twenty shipped on February 25, 1952, to Harper, Reynolds, and Company in Los Angeles.

Figure 32 & inset: Chiefs Special **2928** is in the serial block for the Japanese order.

On the off chance an earlier ramp sight exists I share this. A one-thread *Smith & Wesson Forum* poster put up photos of Chiefs Special serial number **2452**. It had a ramp sight and had been painted over rust. The cylinder had no serial number: a replacement? I asked him if the barrel's serial number matched. He did not reply. I wondered whether the barrel with its ramp sight was also a replacement. We may never know for sure. S&W shipped it to Jennison Hardware Company in Bay City, Michigan, on January 17, 1952.

Smith & Wesson Forum members subtly infused a quirk into me: I must own a S&W shipped in my birth year, birth month, or on my birthday. I caved to the *great enablers'* influence and began the hunt. I started to believe S&W's shipping department shut down in June 1952, then I saw serial number **6634**, with its second flat thumbpiece, one of twenty-one "for various police departments" shipped to George F. Cake Company, Berkeley, California, on June 12, 1952 (Figure 33 & inset). My database now lists 420 Chiefs known to have shipped in 1952, but I have seen only three of the sixty-three shipped in June, including **4875** and **9019**.

Figure 33: Birth month and year Chiefs Special **6634**. Inset: Second flat thumbpiece.

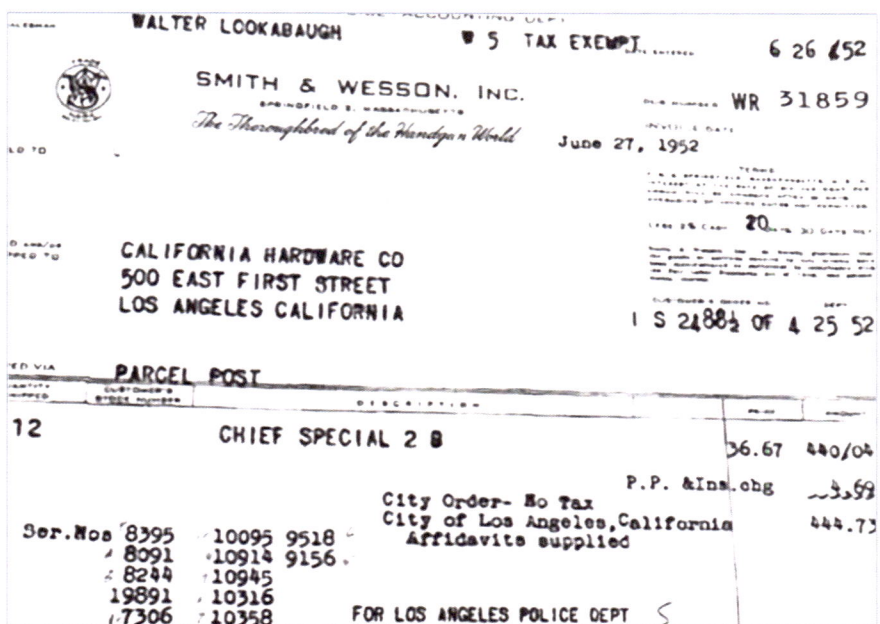

Figure 34: Invoice for 12 LAPD "Chief Special." Check out the wild serial range: 7306-19891. I cropped off the bottom of the invoice and moved the text "FOR LOS ANGELES POLICE DEPT" back into view. (Courtesy of Dr. Roy Jinks)

Dr. Jinks sent this birthday invoice to me (Figure 34). I have not seen one of the twelve 2" blue Chiefs S&W sent to California Hardware Company for the Los Angeles Police Department (LAPD).

A worn Chiefs Special got a makeover (Figures 35-38). My first 1952 Chiefs Special shipped in September, serial number **11920**. Friends used their talents to breathe life into my *Vanity Chiefs Special*: refinished with Cerekote, fresh case-hardening on trigger and bobbed hammer, checked back strap, and relieved trigger guard. Craig Spegel made the Macassar ebony boot stocks and inset my $5 gold piece from 2000.

Figures 35 & 36: Ceramic Cerekote finish, bobbed hammer, checked back strap.

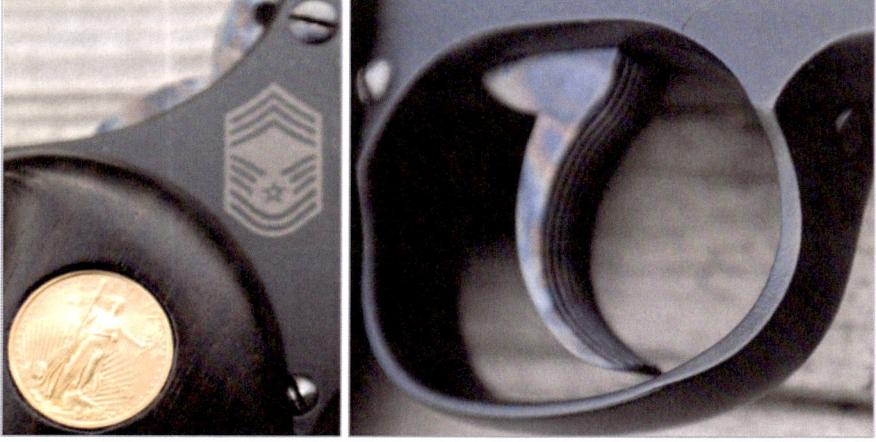

Figures 37 & 38: United States Air Force Chief Master Sergeant stripes, $5 gold piece from my retirement year, new colorful case-hardening, and relieved trigger guard.

S&W identified a Chiefs Special slated to receive a nickel finish by stamping an N on up to three places on the revolver: left of the serial number on the bottom of the barrel, aligned below the serial number on the back of the cylinder beneath the extractor, and lower left side of the grip frame (Figures 39-41).

Figure 39: N stamped on bottom of barrel.

Figure 40: N stamped on back of cylinder.

Figure 41: N stamped on lower left side of grip frame.

The last known Chiefs Special with a smooth ramp front sight shipped in August 1952, serial number **12750**. The first known serrated ramp front sight model shipped in July 1952, serial number **6541**. Smith & Wesson shipped nickel Chiefs Special serial number **14560**, my first with a serrated ramp front sight, to Harvan Sporting Goods Company in New York City on September 25, 1952 (Figure 42 & inset).

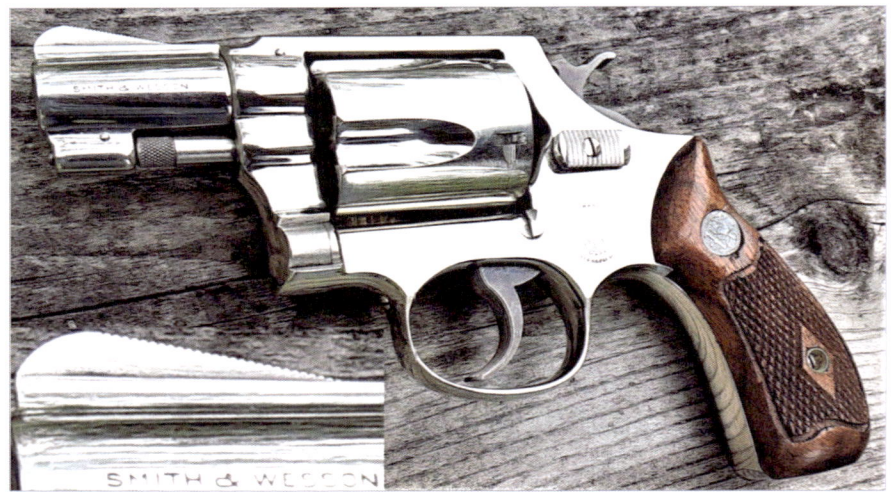

Figure 42: Nickel Chiefs Special **14560**. Inset: Serrated ramp front sight.

Before World War II S&W stamped a B ahead of serial numbers on the barrel of revolvers to be finished in blue. No known Chiefs have a B stamp. We see a fair few refinished nickel Chiefs with no N stamps.

S&W introduced a square butt Chiefs Special in October 1952 at serial number **21342**. A collector said S&W made twenty-five square butt five-screw Chiefs Specials, but I do not know the basis for his claim. My database lists serial numbers **X58**, **X59**, **21342**, and **31899**.

The invoice for "Chief Special" serial number **225** says it has an "oversize trigger guard," and it went to S&W's Superintendent Bill Gunn on September 4, 1951. S&W continued to develop the aluminum alloy 2" Chiefs Special Airweight in 1952, and it became the first production model J-frame with a longer, oval trigger guard. The design eliminated the trigger guard screw, a Smith & Wesson first, making it the first full production four-screw J-frame revolver (Figure 43, *right*). Another change added ⅛" in length to the round butt grip frame.

Figure 43: *Left*: Five-screw J-frame: round trigger guard, short grip frame. *Right*: Four-screw J-frame: oval trigger guard and ⅛" longer round butt grip frame.

S&W produced the first full production Chiefs Special Airweights in the 24000-serial range. S&W shipped seven consecutively numbered **24002-24008** on October 2, 1952, to the United States Marine Corps in Quantico, Virginia. I saw serial number **24004** sell at auction in 2018.

Smith & Wesson engraved *Flora Mitchell Van Orden* on the side plate of Chiefs Special Airweight serial number **24298**, installed smooth rosewood presentation stocks, and shipped it to her Evaluators Limited Gun Shop on February 11, 1953 (Figure 44 & inset). The caliber stamped on the barrel below AIRWEIGHT reads 38 SPECIAL CTG.

Figure 44: Flora (Mitchell) Van Orden's four-screw Chiefs Special Airweight **24298**. Inset: *Flora Mitchell Van Orden* engraved in a single line of calligraphic style script.

Figure 45 shows Flora Van Orden (*center*) holding her Airweight in a photo that came to me with her revolver (photographer unknown).

Figure 45: *Left* to *Right*: Nathan Hoffman, Flora and George Van Orden.

Flora Van Orden is also wearing her Airweight's Berns-Martin shoulder rig in the photo (Figure 46 & inset).

Figure 46: Flora Van Orden's Berns-Martin shoulder holster. Inset: Stampings on the holster's back: C-SPL & BERNS-MARTIN EVALUATORS LTD. QUANTICO, VA.

Observations suggest Smith & Wesson produced at least 500 units in the first Chiefs Special Airweight production run. Smith & Wesson engraved *M.V.W.C.* on serial number **24199** and shipped it to Mrs. Mary Victoria (Wesson) Craw in Charlottesville, Virginia, on February 11, 1953. Mary Craw's dad was former S&W Treasurer Frank H. Wesson. President Hellstrom filed for the Airweight trademark on May 20, 1953, and the United States Patent Office registered it on February 16, 1954.

A wide gap separates serial numbers **52**, the last of the five-screw 3" Chiefs Specials S&W shipped to members of the Joint Brazil-United States Military Commission, and **29863**, the next known five-screw 3" Chiefs Special, which did not ship until May 1955. Smith & Wesson shipped serial numbers **30375**, **30547**, and one more—the next known 3" "Chiefs Special" to ship after serial number **52**—to Charles Greenblatt Company in New York City on July 17, 1953. The invoice also lists five square butt "Chiefs Special." I do not know total production for the five-screw 3" Chiefs. My database lists thirty-seven, and they comprise a wee bit more than two percent of known five-screw Chiefs Specials.

I rescued 3" Chiefs Special serial number **30375**—a rusty relic it was (Figure 47). It also had a broken hammer spur (inset). Ever since I had learned 3" five-screw Chiefs Specials existed, I wanted one. This one, the first one I had seen for sale, joined the herd.

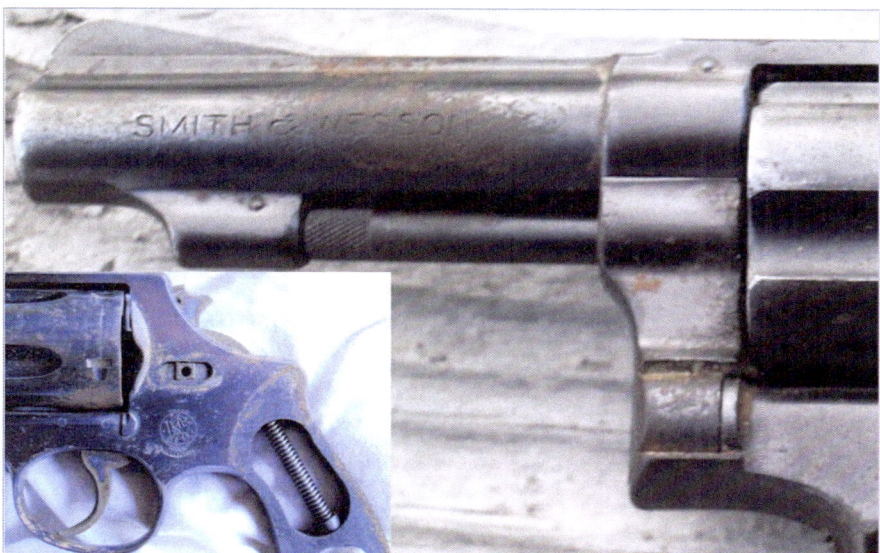

Figure 47: Rust on 3" Chiefs Special **30375**. Inset: Broken hammer spur and rust on the rear left side of the Chiefs Special. Heck of a way to treat it.

I made a rookie mistake right off. The thumbpiece screw broke when I attempted to put it back in after taking it out to clean the gun. I stopped fiddling with it until I could learn from the experts how to handle the neglected little revolver. A *Smith & Wesson Forum* member suggested soaking it in equal parts of automatic transmission fluid and acetone. I mixed the pink potion in a glass, one-gallon pickle jar. The relic soaked for thirty days and emerged rust free. Pure magic.

Adhering to more great advice, I polished it with bronze wool. Then I replaced the hammer and thumbpiece screw and added a small Tyler T-Grip Adapter (Figure 48 and inset). It's a great little shooter and has become my favorite Chiefs Special.

Figure 48: 3" Chiefs Special **30375**. Inset: Barrel caliber reads 38 S.&W. SPECIAL CTG.

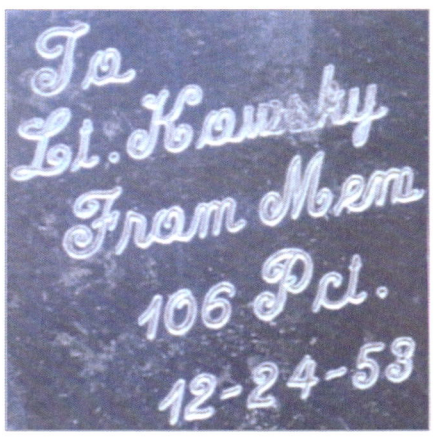

Members of the New York Police Department's 106th precinct in Queens, New York City, engraved the side plate and apparently gave 3" Chiefs Special serial number **30375** to Lieutenant Kowsky on the Eve of Christmas 1953 (Figure 49).

Figure 49: Inscribed side plate.

Smith & Wesson shipped Chiefs Special Airweight serial number **27621** to Rex Firearms Company in New York City on July 31, 1953 (Figure 50). Thanks to its aluminum alloy frame and cylinder, the Chiefs Special Airweight weighs 10¾ ounces.

Figure 50: Four-screw Chiefs Special Airweight **27621**.

Figure 51: Square butt Chiefs Special Airweight **29562**. Inset: Bug screw and its retainer.

Chiefs Special Airweights have steel barrels and yokes. S&W made 3,777 with aluminum cylinders; 923 of those have a square butt. Square butt production began on March 6, 1953, with 2" and 3" barrels. I have not seen an early Airweight with a 3" barrel. Chiefs Special Airweight serial number **29562** shipped in October 1953 (Figure 51). Dr. Jinks said workers called the upper side plate screw the "bug screw" because they said it was a *bugger* to install. It would back its way out of the thin alloy side plate so S&W installed a tiny retainer screw to hold it in place (inset). Retainer screws began to appear on some Airweights shipped in June 1953. Aluminum cylinders were known to rupture so S&W switched to a steel cylinder in January 1954, upping the Airweight to 12½ ounces.

Serial number **42829** was one of three 3" Chiefs Specials in the order, and S&W shipped it to Rex Firearms Company in New York City on May 7, 1954 (Figure 52). It wears a third flat thumbpiece—⅜" tall, ten ridges, eleven valleys, and a new raised ramp at the front (inset).

Figure 52: 3" Chiefs Special **42829**. Inset: Third flat thumbpiece.

Chiefs Special serial number **36722** wears the last known second flat thumbpiece, and it shipped on September 10, 1953. Chiefs Special Airweight serial number **28799**, wearing the first known third flat thumbpiece, shipped in December 1953. The flat thumbpieces exhibit a significant departure from Smith & Wesson's norm, and clearly the company committed itself to producing a functional cylinder release while clinging to the reason it used flat thumbpieces in the first place, whatever the reason. I have not seen an official statement of purpose for the part. Dr. Jinks believes it was a cost-saving measure. Others have speculated it might have eased concealment for off-duty police officers.

The last known carbon steel five-screw 2" Chiefs Special, serial number **45963**, the highest serial number of five in the order, shipped to Warner Hardware Company in Minneapolis, Minnesota, for the City of Minneapolis Police Department on April 30, 1954.

The last known carbon steel five-screw 3" Chiefs Special, serial number **45962**, one of fifteen in the order, shipped on May 27, 1954, to California Hardware Company in Los Angeles. The shipment included eight with higher serial numbers, up to **46025**, but without seeing them I will not guess at whether they have five- or four-screw frames.

Subtracting an estimated number of four-screw Chiefs Special Airweights produced during this era, I calculated Smith & Wesson might have made about 40,000 carbon steel five-screw Chiefs.

Dr. Jinks sent an email to me on December 8, 2022. The email included an attachment he had run across while doing other research. The email's subject read, "Interesting Invoice" (Figure 53). Yes, indeed.

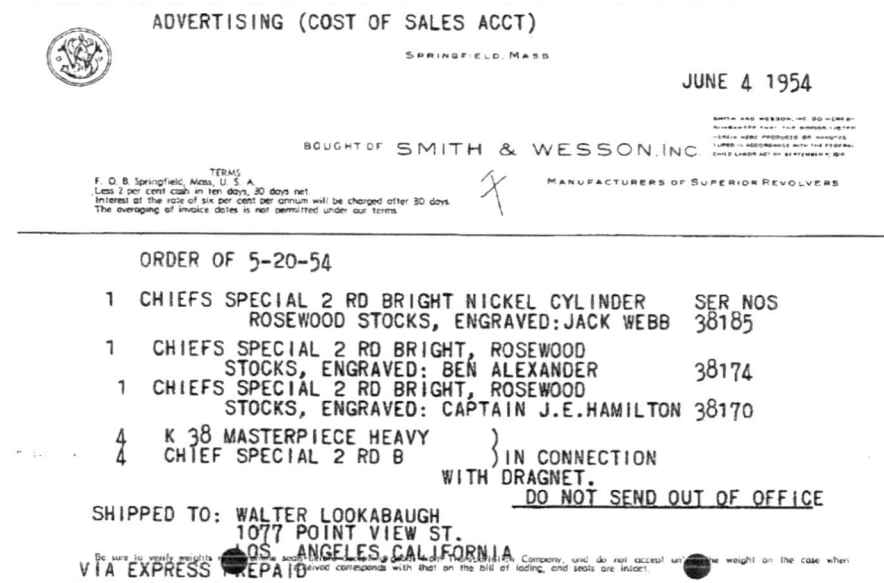

Figure 53: **DRAGNET** invoice. (Courtesy of Dr. Roy Jinks)

Smith & Wesson shipped three inscribed five-screw Chiefs Specials with 2" barrels, round butts, special finishes, and rosewood stocks; four K-38 Masterpieces; and four plain-vanilla Chiefs to its Los Angeles sales representative Walter Lookabaugh. He presented the revolvers to the **DRAGNET** crew.

Jack Webb conjured up Sergeant Joe Friday, an LAPD crime investigator, for his 1949 **DRAGNET** radio show. The radio program aired through 1957. Webb also starred in all 276 **DRAGNET** television episodes from 1951 to 1959. Friday carried LAPD Sergeant shield 714. Ben Alexander played Officer Frank Smith, Friday's partner, and LAPD Captain James E. Hamilton served as **DRAGNET**'s technical adviser.[4]

S&W Collectors Association friend Francis Zandome sent an email with a familiar subject, "For your database," to me on December 3, 2023: His note included an online advertisement for a bright blue, five-screw Chiefs Special with its side plate inscribed *BEN ALEXANDER* (Figure 54). He did not say if he had set his sights on Ben's Chiefs Special so I asked. "No interest," he replied. I clicked the Buy Now button.

Figure 54: S&W gave Chiefs Special serial number **38174** to Ben Alexander. (Photo taken sans right aftermarket stock because it covers BEN.)

The gentleman who works at the shop where I bought Ben's gun agreed to ask the local seller to call me. The seller told me in 1928 his grandfather founded an auction house in Los Angeles. He bought the belongings of entire estates: pots, pans, dishes, furnishings, books, clothes, guns, and all. He told me, "Dad inherited the business, and I worked there when Dad bought Ben Alexander's estate." Ben Alexander passed away on July 5, 1969. The seller said. "I'd stare at Ben's gun sitting

on the corner of Dad's desk. One day Dad asked me, 'Do you want it?'"
He served as the caretaker of Ben's Chiefs Special for fifty-four years.

Ben's gun came to me exactly as the seller had gotten it, with an
Ed Lewis holster (Figure 55) and custom stocks. I had believed LAPD
match shooter "Fuzzy" Farrant made the bird's-eye maple stocks, but a
Smith & Wesson Forum member set me straight. He said: "The grips on
Ben Alexander's Chiefs Special are by Joe Blackford, who was also an
LAPD match shooter. The slope at the recoil shoulder and the pointy finger
grooves are ID features." Other Joe Blackford trademark features include
a pinky rest and an ebony escutcheon nut cover (Figures 56 & 57).[5]

Figure 55:
Ed Lewis holster.

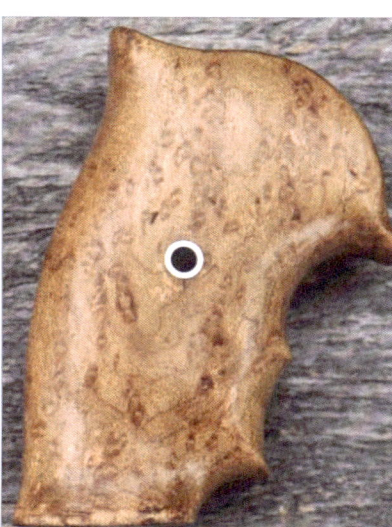

Figures 56 & 57:
Joe Blackford
bird's-eye maple
stocks.

Smith & Wesson Collectors Association friend Tom Horwedel had been paring down his collection and periodically sent a list of Chiefs he'd consider selling. His latest list included Jack Webb's Chiefs Special so I inquired. Tom sent fifteen photos of the revolver and things included with it—along with a price. A few days passed. I could not pass it up.

Dr. Jinks' history letter for Jack Webb's gun says, "This revolver was shipped with a 2 inch barrel, bright blue finish on frame and barrel and nickel plate cylinder ... for presentation to Mr. Jack Webb who starred in the TV series 'Dragnet'." Dr. Jinks went on to say, "Ben Alexander received serial number 38174, he starred as Sergeant Friday's partner, and Captain J. E. Hamilton received serial number 38170 and he worked as an adviser."

LAPD Chief of Police William H. Parker presented a real LAPD Sergeant shield, number 714, to Jack Webb in the 1950s.[6]

The invoice shows Smith & Wesson put rosewood stocks on Jack Webb's engraved, two-tone Chiefs Special. His Chiefs Special flaunts its original rosewood presentation stocks (Figure 58). Smith & Wesson Collectors Association friend Larry Bennett let me use his photo of his exact replica of the shield Chief Parker presented to Jack Webb (inset).

Figure 58: Jack Webb's two-tone five-screw Chiefs Special. Inset: Exact replica of Jack Webb's LAPD shield. (Courtesy of Larry Bennett)

I found this autographed 1960 photo of Ben Alexander (Figure 59). Jack Webb's gun came with his photo, on which he had inscribed a note to LAPD Press Relations Officer Dan Cooke (Figure 60). (Typical of great Hollywood publicity photos, the photographers are not known.)

Figure 59: Ben Alexander.   Figure 60: Jack Webb.

The invoice, Dr. Jinks' letter, and especially the seller's story light the path Ben Alexander's Chiefs Special took to reach me. Those two documents plus additional rich provenance chronicle the coincidental, convergent course Jack Webb's Chiefs Special followed.

Jack Webb passed away on December 23, 1982. His wife Opal gave his Chiefs Special to LAPD's Press Relations Officer Dan Cooke.[7] The two became friends while Dan Cooke served as the adviser for Jack Webb's 1960s **DRAGNET** television series. Dan Cooke passed in 1999. His wife Jane documented the chain of custody for Jack Webb's gun in a letter to an auctioneer. Tom Horwedel won the auction.

The forty-by-eighteen-inch poster for Warner Brothers' 1954 **DRAGNET** movie is my favorite piece of memorabilia to accompany Jack Webb's Chiefs Special (Figure 61). A newspaper clipping announcing Dan Cooke's retirement shows the poster hanging in his LAPD office.

DRAGNET–the movie starring Jack Webb, Ben Alexander, and Richard Boone–premiered in New York City and Chicago in August 1954, and Warner Brothers released it on September 4, 1954.[8]

Actor Richard Boone played Captain James Hamilton in the movie. Captain Hamilton's character did not appear in the television shows.

As an aside, Jack Webb had given his LAPD badge 714 to Dan Cooke. Jane Cooke gave the badge to the Los Angeles Police Academy Museum. It's now at home in the Los Angeles Police Museum.[9]

The museum's curator told me they don't have Captain Hamilton's Chiefs Special.

There's hope!

Figure 61:
1954 *DRAGNET* movie poster. (Licensed for use.)

I found this exceptional example of the 1954 ten-by-eight-inch *DRAGNET* movie poster Warner Brothers sent to movie theaters along with the movie reels "For display in connection with the exhibition of this picture at your theater." It is serial number 54 of 406 (Figure 62).

Figure 62: Warner Brothers' 1954 *DRAGNET* movie poster. Ben Alexander as Officer Frank Smith (*left*), Jack Webb as Sergeant Joe Friday (*right*), and Richard Boone as Captain James Hamilton (*back to camera*) in the movie. (Licensed for use.)

Reuniting Jack Webb's and Ben Alexander's Chiefs Specials set a new high-water mark for my collection in 2024. They presumably had not been together for almost seventy years—since Walter Lookabaugh had presented the pair to the actors in 1954 (Figure 63). I placed a want-to-buy ad on the *Smith & Wesson Forum*, hoping to find an appropriate pair of rosewood stocks for Ben Alexander's gun. No one seemed to have the small rosewood stocks, but a Smith & Wesson Collectors Association friend had an interesting pair of smooth laminated DymondWood stocks from the era.[10] Close enough for now.

Figure 63: The pair of Chiefs Specials Smith & Wesson presented to Jack Webb and Ben Alexander, the two actors who starred in the 1950s **DRAGNET** radio programs, television shows, and the 1954 movie.

Dr. Jinks searched thousands of serial numbers looking for the unadorned Chiefs on **DRAGNET**'s invoice. In February 2024 he found **46289**, **46301**, **46469**, and **46472**. If only I'd known! I let **46289** get away in an April 2023 auction. It went for peanuts. It has the new carbon steel four-screw frame.

Smith & Wesson first shipped four-screw Chiefs Special Airweight models in October 1952, but Smith & Wesson's June 4, 1954, **DRAGNET** invoice reflects the first known ship date for carbon steel four-screw Chiefs Specials–the four plain-vanilla Chiefs Specials Dr. Jinks found for the **DRAGNET** invoice. The invoice also includes the only known mixed shipment of carbon steel Chiefs with five- and four-screw frames, but it does not tell us the number of frame screws on any of the Chiefs. We must see the revolvers to know.

S&W's last known shipment of carbon steel five-screw Chiefs in serial range 29863-30560 filled an order for ten blue 3" Chiefs Specials to Thurman Randall & Company in Dallas, Texas, on May 7, 1955, a year after S&W shipped the five-screw Chiefs Special with the highest known serial number. I have not seen any of the ten 3" Chiefs in the shipment, but based on their serial range I presume they have five-screw frames.

- -

Wouldn't I like to find these needles from this era's haystack?

1) George O. Van Orden's serial number **70**

2) Nickel with a ⅒" service type front sight

3) Nickel with a ⅒" smooth ramp front sight

4) Airweight with a five-screw frame

5) At least one of the twelve Chiefs on my birthday invoice

6) Blue or nickel, five-screw frame, square butt

7) Airweight: square butt, 3" barrel, aluminum cylinder

8) Nickel, five-screw frame, 3" barrel, if one exists

9) Captain J. E. Hamilton's serial number **38170**

10) At least one of the plain-vanilla **DRAGNET** Chiefs

11) At least one of the 3" Chiefs on the May 7, 1955, invoice

To be true to one's own freedom is, in essence,
to honor and respect the freedom of all others.
—Dwight D. Eisenhower

Chapter 3

1954-1958

.38 Chiefs Special
      Carbon steel four-screw
      Aluminum alloy Airweight three-screw
      Carbon steel three-screw

In a bit more than three years Smith & Wesson had reconfigured its five-screw Model J into the four-screw Chiefs Special with a larger, oval trigger guard and ⅛" longer grip frame. Those two features have stood firm as J-frame norms for more than seven decades. The serrated ⅒" wide front sight continued as standard for almost forty years. Chiefs Special Airweights had led the way with major changes during their first era and do again through this period as Smith & Wesson continuously improved its manufacturing efficiency, enhanced performance features, and refined aesthetic characteristics.

In addition to the unadorned **DRAGNET** Chiefs other known carbon steel four-screw Chiefs Specials shipped in June 1954 include serial numbers **46319**, **46448**, and **47169**—the first known four-screw Chiefs Special with a 3" barrel. A Smith & Wesson Collectors Association friend owns blue Chiefs Special serial number **46042**, the first known four-screw Chiefs Special, which shipped in September 1954.

The first four nickel four-screw Chiefs I've documented went to the Turkish Military Attaché in Washington, D.C. The first known carbon steel four-screw Chiefs Special with a nickel finish to stay in the U.S.A. is serial number **47475** (Figure 64). Cylinder and grip frame have N stamps, but it's a wee bit odd the matching-serial number barrel does not. Smith & Wesson delivered it to S&W Sales Manager Harold Austin on August 30, 1954. Typical of Chiefs given to Smith & Wesson's staff, the invoice says he would use it "for demonstration purposes." It sports an odd fourth flat thumbpiece with an unusual seven ridges and eight valleys (inset). I have also seen the same thumbpiece on nickel four-screw Chiefs with serial numbers **47488** and **48403**, shipped in July 1954, and on nickel I-frame 1953 .22/32 Kit Gun serial number 3553.

Figure 64: Nickel Chiefs Special **47475** given to S&W Sales Manager Harold O. Austin. Inset: Only seen in nickel the fourth flat thumbpiece has seven ridges and eight valleys.

Blue Chiefs continued to wear the third flat thumbpiece with ten ridges. It's seen here on 3" Chiefs Special serial number **50865**, shipped to the Honolulu Sports Company in Honolulu, Territory of Hawaii, on February 4, 1955 (Figure 65). It has a satin blue finish, small hammer, four-screw frame, and the third flat thumbpiece (inset).

Figure 65: 3" Chiefs Special **50865**. Inset: Third flat thumbpiece.

Many Chiefs Special Airweights in the 52600-54200 serial range shipped out of sequence. Serial number **52620** shipped in February 1955 and wears the first known fifth flat thumbpiece: back to eleven ridges and twelve valleys with a more angled ramp. Others in the serial range with known ship dates shipped between April 1956 and December 1957. The company abbreviated the caliber on the right side of the barrel to 38 SPL. CTG. These Airweights introduced S&W's three-screw side plate: *away* with the bothersome bug and retainer screws!

S&W shipped Chiefs Special Airweight serial number **60625** on April 1, 1955, to M. & H. Sporting Goods Company in Philadelphia, Pennsylvania (Figure 66). It has matching-serial number diamond magna stocks. The screw holding the new fifth flat thumbpiece in place spans ridges four through six and reaches into the left slope of the seventh ridge. Milling variations exist, making this thumbpiece a challenge to distinguish from its successor when seen from the face. Atop the side plate's inside wall, a tongue slips into a notch in the frame to secure the side plate to the frame, eliminate bug and retainer screws, and pioneer a new standard for Smith & Wesson's small-framed revolvers (inset).

Figure 66: Chiefs Special Airweight **60625**. Inset: three-screw side plate with tongue.

S&W shipped four-screw 3" Chiefs Special serial number **59221** to Sutcliff Hardware Company in Louisville, Kentucky, on April 8, 1955. (Figure 67). It has the new fifth flat thumbpiece.

Figure 67: 3" Chiefs Special **59221**. Matching-serial numbered right stock.

Smith & Wesson shipped the twelfth known nickel Chiefs Special with a four-screw frame, serial number **63331**, on May 26, 1955, to H. H. Harris Company in Chicago, Illinois. It shipped as one of ten in the order. (Figure 68). It has the expected three N stamps on the bottom of the barrel, back of the cylinder, and lower left side of the grip frame. The serial number on its right stock matches the one on the butt, and it wears the same fifth flat thumbpiece as its blue siblings (inset).

Figure 68: Nickel Chiefs Special **63331**. Inset: Fifth flat thumbpiece.

JA38, S&W's internal code for the Chiefs Special Airweight, set a precedent. Dr. Jinks told me Engineering Change #168 on December 13, 1955, said, "Add a tongue to the top of all I, IT [I-frame Target], & J side plates, make the tongue the same as on the JA38 side plate. This will eliminate the bug screw (upper side plate screw) and counter bore and hole." Smith & Wesson shipped serial number **73759**, the first known blue carbon steel three-screw Chiefs Special and one of twenty-five Chiefs in the shipment, to Shapleigh Hardware Company in St. Louis, Missouri, on April 24, 1956.

Engineering Change #463, December 23, 1955, calls for the "shape (side profile) of the [Chiefs' hammer] spur" to be "the same shape as IT22 [1953 .22/32 Kit Gun]," Dr. Jinks said. The first known new large hammer appears on square butt Chiefs Special Airweight serial number **52637**, shipped in June 1956.

A special order, bright blue four-screw 3" Chiefs Special serial number **55693** shipped on May 2, 1956, to Rex Firearms Company in New York City (Figure 69). In 1956 S&W changed from postwar satin blue to a bright blue finish on most revolvers. It has a serial number-matching right stock, and its trigger and small hammer show off their handsome case-hardened colors. Chiefs Special Airweight serial number **77850** has the last known small hammer, and it also shipped in May 1956.

Figure 69: Bright blue finish on Chiefs Special **55693**, my first 3" with a square butt.

About here another obvious hole appears in my herd. Try as I might, I have not found the illusive early carbon steel Chiefs Special with a three-screw frame. I have looked for early ones with a small hammer or a later one with the new large hammer. I am not the only one with this need. Several friends are in search of a Chiefs Special from this era for their collections. The hunt, though, offers at least half the fun.

Smith & Wesson shipped Chiefs Special serial number **93475**, one of twenty-five in the order, to J. L. Galef & Sons Incorporated in New York City on January 11, 1957 (Figure 70). The serial number inside the right stock matches. It's my first with a sixth flat thumbpiece, which I'll define in the next Chapter. It's my only carbon steel Chiefs Special with a three-screw frame, and it's also my first with a large hammer (inset).

Figure 70: Three-screw Chiefs Special serial number **93475**. Inset: Large hammer.

Smith & Wesson eliminated the "soft fitting" production process in 1957. The change's most noticeable effect phased out stamping serial numbers on the bottom of the barrel, back of the cylinder, and back of the yoke approximately between Chiefs Special serial numbers 90000 and 125000. Examples within this range have appeared with one, two, three, or none of these parts stamped with a serial number. The company's improved manufacturing processes simultaneously did away with the soft fitting step and the need for the three serial numbers.

Smith & Wesson stopped pre-fitting and dismantling the parts before a revolver's one and only assembly. Dr. Jinks told me it was a long process because it required retraining a lot of people, including the fitters, assemblers, and inspectors, on the new methods of producing guns using finished parts. He added that this new thinking also put pressure on the company to ensure it did not adversely affect quality.

Other distinct production details also had to change to complete the process. For example, Dr. Jinks sent Engineering Change #501 from April 24, 1957, to me; it calls for the thickness of the hand on all frame sizes to be altered, and the "Reason for change" listed on the engineering change said, "More efficient method of assembly under New Method." Seeing this order led me to believe there must have been other nuances the company would have addressed to fully implement its plan.

On June 12, 1957, S&W assigned model numbers to adjoin the original model names of its handguns. The carbon steel Chiefs Special added **Model 36,** and alloy Chiefs Special Airweights added **Model 37**. The change took quite some time to show up on the street.

Smith & Wesson printed its first catalog to show model numbers in March 1958. S&W printed the first invoice to list a model number at the end of the model description on April 9, 1958. Then on April 14 the model number appeared at the beginning and end of the description. On April 15 the model number hung on at the beginning of the description, becoming the new factory standard. Dr. Jinks told me this all happened months before S&W began stamping model numbers on its revolvers.

Higher serial numbers appear on invoices with earlier dates, but Chiefs Special serial number **126513** shipped in July 1958, and it's the last known carbon steel Chiefs Special sans model number.

The highest known serial number for a Chiefs Special Airweight without a model number is **131845**. The invoice identifies it as "M37," and it shipped to the George F. Cake Company in Berkeley, California, on June 17, 1958. Chiefs Special Airweight serial number **130794** shipped on August 22, 1958, to Monroe Hardware Company in Monroe, North Carolina (Figure 71). It does not have a model number, and the assembly number on its frame moved from the yoke cut to the new location on the lower left side of the grip frame (inset).

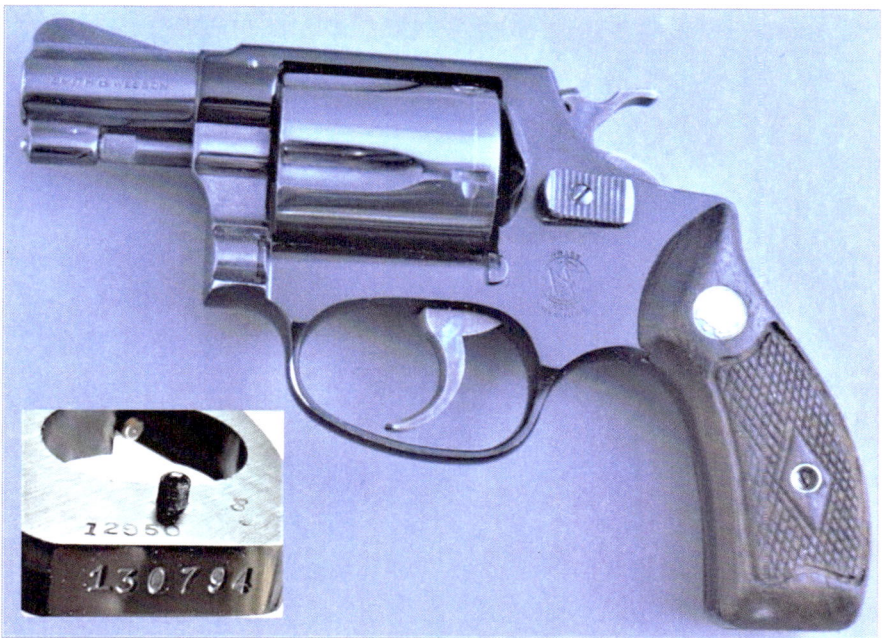

Figure 71: Chiefs Special Airweight **130794** sans Model 37 stamp. Inset: Frame assembly number in its new location on the lower left side of the grip frame.

A variety of theories explain the cause of an Airweight revolver problem. The aluminum frame cracks in the thin area beneath where the barrel protrudes into the frame. Some say it comes from overtightening the barrel during assembly, and some blame it on using hot ammo. Who knows for sure? None of my Airweights' frames have a crack so I do not have an image of the phenomenon.

An Airweight's cracked frame cannot be repaired so the gun ends up as a parts gun or a paperweight, albeit a light one. Known examples tell of Smith & Wesson replacing a cracked Airweight with a new revolver.

- -

Wouldn't I like to find these Chiefs Specials from this era?

1) Chiefs Special, three-screw frame, serial range 73xxx-78xxx, small or large hammer

2) Chiefs Special, serial range 126xxx, not model marked

We must be free not because we claim
freedom, but because we practice it.
—William Faulkner

Chapter 4

1958-1964

.38 Chiefs Special
    Carbon steel Model 36
    Aluminum alloy Airweight Model 37

The first known Chiefs Special Model 36, serial number **126017**, shipped to L. H. Kurtz Company in Des Moines, Iowa, on September 4, 1958, my third day in Mrs. Miller's first-grade class (Figure 72). The ship date is also the earliest known Model 36 ship date. It wears handsome aftermarket Sambar stag grips. MOD-36 appears beneath the frame's assembly number in the yoke cut (inset). No other known Chiefs Specials, Models 36 or 37, have assembly and model numbers stamped together, rather we see model numbers stamped on the frame in the yoke cut, and assembly numbers stamped in the new location on the lower left side of the grip frame.

Figure 72: First known 2" Chiefs Special Model 36 serial number **126017**.
Inset: Assembly and model numbers stamped on the frame in the yoke cut.

Smith & Wesson Collectors Association friend Jim DeMarco owns the first known Chiefs Special Airweight Model 37, serial number **129851**. It and Model 37 serial numbers **131665** and **141326** shipped on October 10, 1958, to Morley Brothers Company in Saginaw, Michigan. The earliest known Model 37 ship date is September 1958, serial number **130774**, and it's owned by another friend who's a member of the Smith & Wesson Collectors Association.

S&W shipped the first known 3" Chiefs Special Model 36, serial number **133998**, to Lawrence E. Bogert in Sandusky, Ohio, on October 20, 1958 (Figure 73). The invoice shows five "M36" Chiefs with 2" barrels and five with 3" barrels.

Figure 73: First known 3" Chiefs Special Model 36 **133998**.

Please don't do to your Chiefs what somebody did to this poor Model 36 (Figure 74 and inset in the cylinder window). We will never know why or how, but I saw it and knew I had to attempt another rescue. I removed the stocks but did not try to turn another screw.

Figure 74: Note the vanquished four lines of text on the frame. Inset: MOD-36 stamp.

Model 36 serial number **138852** began life when Smith & Wesson shipped it to Piedmont Hardware Company in Danville, Virginia, on January 9, 1959. Its serial number-matching walnut magna stocks show little checking, and only a hint remains of the diamonds (Figure 75).

Figure 75: Left and right stocks showing their wear and serial number **138852**.

Its cylinder spun freely in the yoke when I rolled it out. When it was back in place, sometimes it locked up, but it rarely rotated when I cocked the hammer. On a good note the hammer locked firm when cocked and could not be pushed off. Experience had taught me it needed to soak in an automatic transmission fluid and acetone bath before I tried to turn another screw. It began to soak on November 16, 2024, and it emerged on December 18.

The bare steel had turned dark, and its snubby nose still dripped three days later (Figure 76).

After I gave it a good wipe down the thumbpiece and yoke screws came out with ease. I removed the thumbpiece, yoke, and cylinder without a hitch. The extractor rod then unthreaded with ease, letting me unscrew it from the extractor and pull out its spring and the center pin and spring. Those parts looked nearly new.

The last two screws on the side plate seemed to be welded in position. I needed a Plan B. A friend suggested heating up the frame opposite the screws. As I expected a cheap lighter did not do the trick. Plan C? Perhaps a few days with a gunsmith is what it needs. It sure can start a conversation!

Figure 76: Mistreated Model 36 **138852**.

We don't see great numbers of two-tone Chiefs Specials from the 1950s. Heck, we don't see many from any era. According to Dr. Jinks, Smith & Wesson assembled two-tone revolvers to fill special orders or use leftover parts at the end of a production run. Most have blue frames and might be adorned with a nickel barrel, cylinder, extractor rod, screws, and thumbpiece, but there are no rules. A two-tone may comprise any combination of parts. S&W shipped Chiefs Special Model 36 serial number **158956** to H. L. Peters Incorporated in Buffalo, New York, on May 27, 1959 (Figure 77). It has a blue extractor rod, frame, screws, and the sixth flat thumbpiece with a steeper ramp, eleven ridges, and twelve valleys; its screw's head spans ridges four through six and cuts into the seventh ridge (variations exist) (inset). The nickel barrel and cylinder wear the expected N stamps. S&W made few Chiefs with a two-tone finish so the company did not print special labels for their boxes. Labels on nickel Chiefs Special boxes of this era had red printing. This matching-serial number box's creative labeling sort of hints at what's inside (Figure 78).

Figure 77: Two-tone 3" Model 36 **158956**. The right diamond magna stock's serial number matches the ones on the butt and box. Inset: Sixth flat thumbpiece.

Figure 78: Two-tone label on the box. Note the incorrect singular Chief.

S&W shipped the seventh known nickel 3" Chiefs Special Model 36, serial number **180475**, in February 1961 (Figure 79).

Figure 79: Nickel 3" Chiefs Special Model 36 **180475**.

Smith & Wesson shipped nickel Chiefs Special Model 36 serial number **271969** to Harvan Sporting Goods Company in New York City on December 5, 1962 (Figure 80). I first documented this seventh flat thumbpiece at serial number **204793** in 1961. Its less abrupt ramp is the same height as the last one. It has twelve ridges and thirteen valleys (inset).

Figure 80: Nickel 2" Model 36 **271969**. Inset: Seventh flat thumbpiece.

S&W issued an engineering change on September 12, 1962, to alter how the J-frame's mainspring rod engages the hammer. Dr. Jinks said the change occurred near serial number **295000**. S&W replaced the rod's ball with a stirrup that resembles a two-pronged fork (Figures 81 & 82). A stirrup pin rides in the stirrup. The pin spans the back end of a cupped channel three-quarters the length of the hammer's base.

Figure 81: Ball and socket   Figure 82: Stirrup and pin.

Chiefs maintain model numbers and do not add a suffix to denote an engineering change. Smith & Wesson added a sequential number for each engineering change on most other models, which usually signified the previous model had been replaced (e.g., by 1963 S&W's .44 Magnum Model 29 had become Model 29-2 thanks to two engineering changes). Chiefs Specials experienced engineering changes, but the models dodged engineering change numbers for another quarter century.

In the early 1960s Clara and Frederick Toppan served on the staff at the University of Wyoming in Laramie. Clara co-founded the Toppan Rare Books Library, a delightful, hands-on reference facility located in UW's renowned and historic archive: the American Heritage Center. Active sports shooters, the Toppans built a notable gun collection, which included a number of nice Smith & Wesson revolvers. They bequeathed their collection to the American Heritage Center. In thirty-five years the center had never displayed it. In 2021 UW's board of trustees told the director to liquidate it. UW's lawyers guided him to pick a California pawn shop to erase yet another bit of American and Wyoming heritage.

I found the Toppan's 3" Chiefs Special Model 36 as I searched for Chiefs Specials on an Internet auction site. The pawn shop's owner had used the yoke assembly number as the serial number in the auction's listing. He had no idea the large aftermarket stocks hid the serial number on the gun's butt. Serial number **336411** shipped in April 1964 (Figure 83). The owner told me how he had come to have the Chiefs Special, and he said the Toppans had hired a gunsmith in Jackson Hole, Wyoming, to "go through and enhance" it. The American Heritage Center director told me the proceeds from auctioning off the Toppan collection would help support Clara's library. As expected this Chiefs Special has the new stirrup mainspring rod.

Figure 83: I wrangled the Toppan's Model 36 serial number **336411** back to ol' Wyo. Its visible enhancements include a trigger shoe and Steve Herrett's stocks.

Figure 84: 3" Chiefs Special Airweight Model 37 **366687** with a square butt.

I prefer Chiefs with 3" barrels and square butts. I had a devil of a time finding a 3" Chiefs Special Airweight Model 37 with a square butt. Chiefs Special Airweight serial number **366687** has a square butt and serial number-matching diamond magna stocks. It shipped two weeks after All Hallows' Eve on November 13, 1964, to Leslie Edelman Incorporated in Mount Laurel, New Jersey (Figure 84).

- -

Wouldn't I like to find this Chiefs Special from this era?

Model 36, serial range 180000-201000, with the sixth flat thumbpiece, shipped ~1960

A person who never made a mistake
never tried anything new.
—Albert Einstein

Chapter 5

1964-1969

.38 Chiefs Special
  Carbon steel Models 36 & 36-1
  Aluminum alloy Airweight Model 37
  Stainless steel Model 60

His first year as S&W president, Bill Gunn approved producing a new stainless steel Chiefs Special. Development began in 1964 and production in 1965. S&W merged the stainless models into the Chiefs Special serial number series and completed thirty-nine by summer's end.

Another Smith & Wesson First!

The Handgun has long been plagued by the destructive influence of rust and corrosion.

Smith & Wesson has now broken through this barrier pioneering the use of stainless steel in the favorite undercover gun of Law Enforcement.

This is a preview of our release for October, 1965

Chief
HOW ABOUT THIS?

The .38 Chief's Special

STAINLESS

FOR USE IN AREAS OF HIGH HUMIDITY AND SALT ATMOSPHERE
IN THE INTERIOR – ON THE SEACOAST

SMITH & WESSON
SPRINGFIELD, MASSACHUSETTS, U.S.A.
For Further Details • Write Smith & Wesson • Attention Dept. PH-2

Figure 85: Smith & Wesson's 1965 stockholder report preview and the *Police Chief* Magazine advertisement. (Courtesy of Dr. Roy Jinks and IACP/*Police Chief*)

Smith & Wesson previewed the revolutionary stainless steel .38 Chiefs Special in its August 1965 stockholder report (Figure 85). *Police Chief* Magazine's October 1965 issue carried S&W's full-page ad sans the verbiage above my inset red dashed line. For some unknown reason the Chiefs Special model name became possessive.

Smith & Wesson put a mirror-bright, polished finish on every exposed part of stainless Chiefs Special revolvers. The company made one configuration: a 2" barrel and a round butt. The Smith & Wesson name on the barrel's left side included the traditional S&W ampersand.

Stainless Chiefs Specials wear a contoured thumbpiece, hearkening back to the very first 1950 Model J, serial number **6** (Figure 86).

Figure 86: 1965 stainless steel contoured thumbpiece.

Subtle distinctions include a V stamped on back of the cylinder and Ss stamped on the bottom of the barrel and the lower left side of the grip frame. An observant viewer might infrequently find an anomaly: an S stamped on a trigger's upper left or right side. Did an original trigger fail an inspection, causing a fitter to pull a replacement trigger out of a bin of spare stainless parts and stamped with an S so they couldn't be mistaken for carbon steel parts?

Smith & Wesson Historical Foundation Historian Don Mundell told me early stainless Chiefs' boxes bore a Carpenter Steel Company logo (Figure 87). Don said Roy Jinks told him it was the first time a Smith & Wesson product bore another company's logo.

United States Steel developed the "Steelmark" without text in the 1950s. U.S. Steel later gave the logo to the American Iron and Steel Institute. Companies may ask AISI for permission to use the logo.[11] Say! How 'bout those Pittsburg Steelers?

Figure 87: Carpenter Steel Company logo on the box label of a S&W stainless steel Chiefs Special. Carpenter Steel Company either operates under a new name or is no longer in business.

Smith & Wesson introduced its small carbon steel .38 Special revolver at the International Association of Chiefs of Police conference in October 1950. Chiefs dubbed it the *Chiefs Special*. Next, S&W débuted its J-frame aluminum alloy .38 *Bodyguard* at the chiefs' October 1955 conference in Philadelphia, Pennsylvania. Following those precedents, established when Bill Gunn was S&W's plant superintendent, President Gunn travelled to the chiefs' annual conference at Hotel Fontainebleau in Miami Beach, Florida, October 2-7, 1965, to unveil the world's first regular production stainless handgun: *.38 Chiefs Special Stainless Model 60*.

Smith & Wesson loaned Model 60 serial number **401781** to gun writer L. R. "Bob" Wallack so he could write a magazine article about the new model. Wallack stowed S&W's Memorandum Account M00184 packing list in the original box. The packing list suggests he picked up the gun at the factory on October 21, 1965 (Figure 88). Wallack put the revolver through its paces, then he wrote a product review for a gun magazine. "I read that article when it came out," *Smith & Wesson Forum* owner Lee Jarrett said.

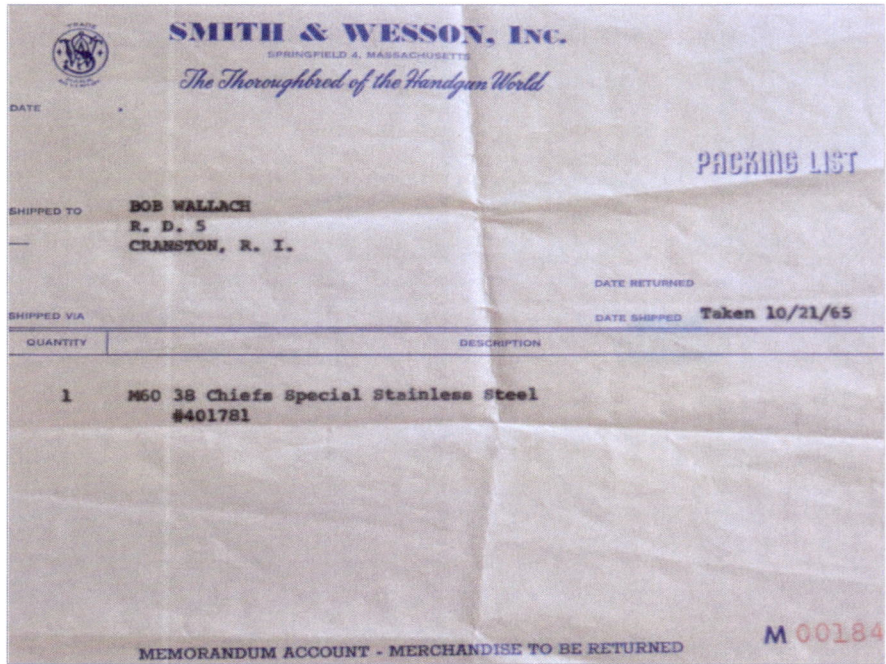

Figure 88: Memorandum Account M 00184 packing list for Model 60 serial number **401781**, Wallack's loaner. What's in a name? His last name is misspelled on the form.

I could not find the article Lee read, but a *Smith & Wesson Forum* member told me about Wallack's book: *American Pistol & Revolver Design and Performance*. In it Wallack tells his story. In one of his photo captions Wallack said, "The first stainless-steel revolver to leave the Smith & Wesson plant was this Model 60 Chief's Special." No, sir, it was not. Dr. Bill Cross said S&W shipped six of twenty stainless Model 15s in 1960.

Plus Dr. Jinks found shipping records for fourteen Model 60s S&W shipped before Wallack picked up his loaner at the plant. S&W shipped eight on October 5, 1965, including serial number **401774** to S&W Treasurer Frank Symonds, two to Olympic Wholesale Company in Los Angeles, and five to S&W's Southern representative Patterson & Hanson Company in Largo, Florida. On October 18, 1965, S&W also shipped six more: serial number **401754** to Sharp-Horsey Hardware Company in Atlanta, Georgia, one to Marble Hardware Company in Wareham, Massachusetts, and four to Charles Greenblatt Company in New York City, which the invoice shows earmarked for the chiefs' conference in Miami Beach, Florida. Had Charles Greenblatt Company dispatched a sales team to the chiefs' Miami Beach conference to take their orders?

Wallack's loaner and the two bold serial numbers in the previous paragraph came from the summer run of thirty-nine revolvers. Research led Dr. Jinks to conclude those serial numbers span serial range 391978-401887. Known carbon steel .38 Chiefs Special Model 36s intermingle with the stainless Chiefs throughout the range. The other twelve stainless Chiefs shipped in October came from the first regular production block of about 900 Model 60s.

Three October-shipped Model 60s have known whereabouts: Tom Schubert shared details about Frank Symonds': It wears smooth rosewood presentation stocks and factory engraving by Tom Freyburger; Wallack's loaner is one of twelve cornerstones in the dodecagonal foundation of my collection; and another Smith & Wesson Collectors Association friend owns the one sent to Marble Hardware Company. My Chiefs Special database lists the fifteen shipped in October, more from the early run, and many from six of the seven regular 1960s Model 60 production runs.

Figure 89 and its inset box ends feature Wallack's loaner with its polished stainless finish. Dr. Jinks' history letter says, "This revolver was from the first production group of 12 units." Note S&W's traditional ampersand on the left side of the barrel. The Model 60's new contoured thumbpiece foretold the end of the fifteen-year evolution of J-frame flat thumbpiece variations.

Figure 89 & insets: Wallack's loaner Model 60 **401781**. *Bottom* inset shows where S&W affixed the Carpenter Steel Company logo.

S&W advertisements said, "Wet, humid conditions that would rust out even the best blued or nickeled gun hardly touch this new S&W .38 Chief's Special STAINLESS, Model 60." Did Wallack interpret the S&W marketing claim as puffery he felt obliged to prove or disprove? He said, "After shooting the gun for a few weeks I thought it would be a good exercise to subject it to something of a torture test to see what would happen." His handwritten note, which he left in the box, explains what he did with Smith & Wesson's property (Figure 90).

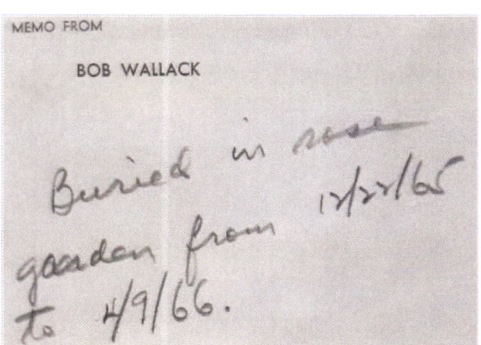

Figure 90: Wallack's note.

Wallack's story gets even better. He followed these steps after he exhumed the new stainless steel Model 60 from its wintery rose garden grave in Rhode Island: "When I dug it up I just washed it off with the garden hose, loaded it, and fired it." He went on to say, "From that day on, as long as I had the gun, it was never cleaned or even oiled. And it never failed to work properly."

Wallack documented one problem he noted after his torture test: "There was a *slight discoloration* [emphasis mine] on the hammer and trigger." He went on to describe his rationale for the discoloration. He believed it was, "The result of a heat treatment of these parts which added carbon to make the parts harder." Has the hammer's condition since worsened?

Still today a gross stain plagues the polished hammer (Figure 91). The trigger appears almost new except for a few black specks on its right side (Figure 92). I have not tried to polish them.

 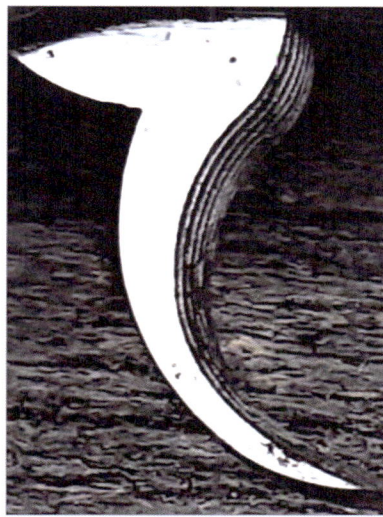

Figure 91: Hammer's stain.   Figure 92: Trigger's specks

Early Model 60 advertisements boasted, "Barrel, frame, cylinder, screws, springs and every part in it, except the walnut stock – are machined from solid stainless steel!" Wallack said, "Even the grips stood the treatment well." The serial numbers stamped inside the right diamond magna stock and on the butt match the serial number on the box of Wallack's Model 60.

I summarized the next snippet of the saga from several personal communications with Dr. Jinks and excerpts from his historical letter. S&W required writers to return loaned guns to the company after they completed an article. At some point Smith & Wesson told Wallack to return the Model 60 or pay for it. He agreed to pay. On October 17, 1971, President Gunn finally gave his approval for Wallack to keep the revolver. Wallack paid the next day.

Wallack also left this handwritten note in the box. He wrote it to Joe on December 22, 1972 (Figure 93 with transcription inset).

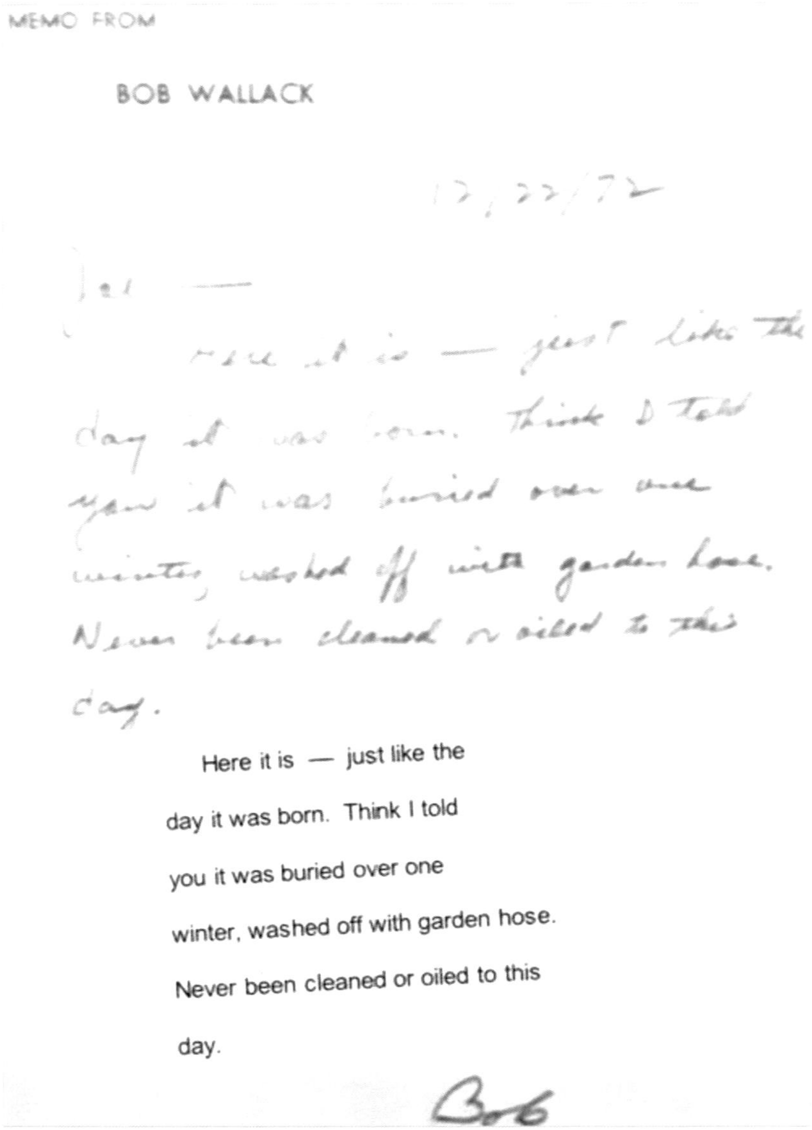
MEMO FROM

BOB WALLACK

12/22/72

Joe —

Here it is — just like the
day it was born. Think I told
you it was buried over one
winter, washed off with garden hose.
Never been cleaned or oiled to this
day.

Here it is — just like the
day it was born. Think I told
you it was buried over one
winter, washed off with garden hose.
Never been cleaned or oiled to this
day.

Bob

Figure 93 & inset: Wallack's note to "Joe."

Wallack's storied stainless Model 60 wound up in the Joseph M. Wanenmacher Jr. collection. Joe Wanenmacher Jr. passed away on February 10, 2022, and his online obituary tells us, "He created the Wanenmacher Arms Show" in Tulsa, Oklahoma.[12] Mr. Wanenmacher's Model 60 went to auction in October 2022.

Now flash back to the evolution of the Smith & Wesson company and its Model 60. The Wesson family had reached an agreement to sell its controlling interest in Smith & Wesson Incorporated to the Bangor Punta Corporation late in 1965.

Dr. Jinks sent a page from S&W's October 1965 catalog, the first to list the .38 Chiefs Special Stainless Model 60. The cost? $85. A blue, carbon steel Chiefs Special Model 36 with a 2" or 3" barrel and round or square butt cost $65, and nickel cost $70 ($5 and $4 higher than the prices listed on the fifteen-year-old Chiefs Special flyer). Chiefs Special Airweight Model 37s in one of four barrel-butt combinations cost $70 for blue or $77 for nickel.

S&W's Engineering Change No. 944, dated January 11, 1966, for "Part Name: Stock" said: "Eliminate Diamond around escutcheon & escutcheon nut; recess escutcheon & escutcheon nut below checking" on "all models," except one changed in October 1965. S&W continued to use the diamond stocks until exhausting its inventory.

In another engineering change S&W replaced the other J-frames' flat thumbpieces with new contoured thumbpieces on February 11, 1966. Studying known shipping dates, I discovered this change appears to have taken place almost overnight.

S&W's catalog shows a $90 price effective March 1, 1966. From the first Model 60 production run S&W shipped serial number **410010** to Hunt & Whitaker Company in Jackson, Mississippi, for the County of Shelby, Tennessee, on March 17, 1966 (Figure 94). The invoice shows a $52.89 wholesale price. Serial numbers match on right stock, gun, and box, the top of which does not bear Bangor Punta's name (inset). Model 60's product brochure shows the "Finish" as "Polished Stainless Steel" (inset). Text on the barrel's left side has a generic ampersand, first noted on some 2" Chiefs Specials in 1963. S&W alternately used the traditional and generic ampersands on its 2" Chiefs for at least the next three years before switching to the generic ampersand as standard.

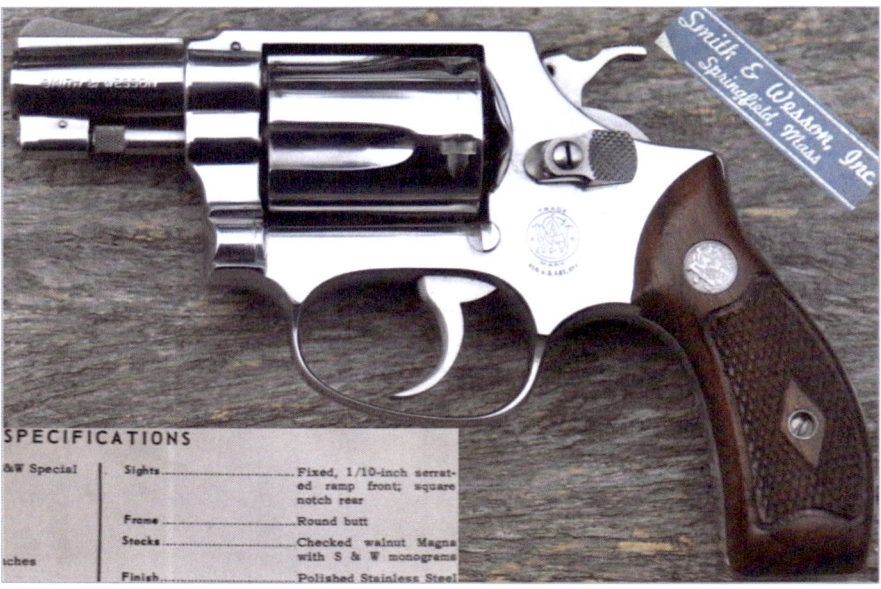

Figure 94: First regular production run Model 60 **410010**. Insets: *Top*: S&W's name on the box top. *Bottom*: Product brochure's Specifications.

In serial order but out of ship-date order, here I am to present my most unusual Chiefs Special—the true pinnacle of my collection. Model 60 serial number **410056** went to Roy G. Jinks on July 12, 1972 (Figure 95).

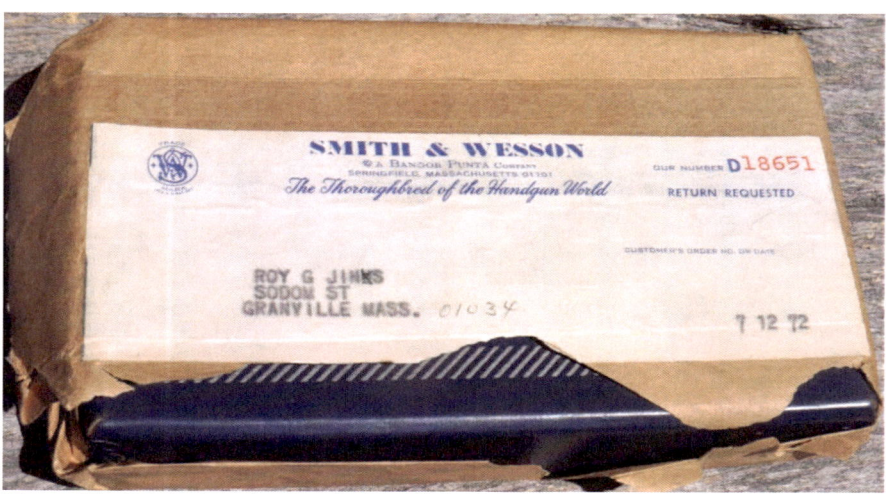

Figure 95: Original packaging for Dr. Jinks' Model 60 serial number **410056**.

Like serial number **410010**, **410056** came from the first regular production run, but it took a path unlike the others. Instead of leaving the plant it went to engineer Don Fogg, and he tried something different.

Don Fogg applied a bright blue finish on the polished stainless steel Model 60. Although the frame in the yoke cut is not stamped Model 60, the requisite S stamps are in place on the bottom of the barrel, lower left side of the grip frame, and even on the yoke. The expected V stamp is also in its usual place on the back of the cylinder. It wears its original polished stainless steel thumbpiece, extractor rod, and center and locking bolt pins, but Fogg blued its barrel pin, screws, and extractor, and he also installed a later flash chromed stainless steel hammer and trigger. A Smith & Wesson Collectors Association friend owns another Model 60 that was given what he called a "black rubber-like finish," the only known example.

According to Dr. Jinks, his Model 60 originally wore matching-serial number diamond magna stocks, but Fogg exchanged those for a pair of banana stocks with a speed loader cutout. Model 60 serial number **410056** resides in a blue box, but there is no printed text on the left end, and it's clear the paper label that's there wasn't completed by the typical inspector-packer team. Its serial number-matching label identifies the Model 60, blue finish, and 2" barrel. The box contains an original tool set, but its product brochure shows a later satin finish. Dr. Jinks returned his Model 60 to Don Fogg. Don passed away in October 2023, and his son complied with Don's wishes to return the gun to Dr. Jinks.

After I acquired Model 60 serial number **401867** Dr. Jinks and I corresponded often. I displayed my Chiefs Special collection at the Smith & Wesson Collectors Association symposium in Glendale, Arizona, in June 2023, and he became more interested as he saw it grow. He humbled me late in 2024 when he told me his blue Model 60 **410056** belonged in my collection. I felt honored, and now, here it is (Figures 96 & 97).

Figure 96: Dr. Jinks' blued stainless steel Model 60 serial number **410056**.

Figure 97: As a standard rule I do not shoot revolver photographs in direct sun, but the magical iridescent qualities of Don Fogg's blued stainless are captivating. The look appears translucent, yet it resembles the effect hot rod painters achieve when they add glittery particles to pearlescent paint. The appearance morphs from metalflake blues to browns.

Many new products born of great ideas experience growing pains. Does the problem exacerbate when a company itself experiences a state of flux? After learning of a problem with the Model 60 Smith & Wesson developed a solution. In his book Dr. Jinks reported, "The material used in the hammer & trigger was not sufficiently hardened." He clarified the problem in a February 2023 email: "The triggers and hammers were made of stainless steel, however, the stainless could not be hardened enough to prevent the tip of the trigger release and the hammer notches from rounding, causing the gun not to function properly." The two earliest Model 60s in my collection continue to function properly.

In his book Dr. Jinks explained Smith & Wesson first solved the problem of "not sufficiently hardened" stainless hammers and triggers by case-hardening them, "producing a dark finish." The first production run's Model 60s with late 1966 ship dates began to show up with dull, monochrome hammers and triggers, ranging from dark bronze or dark gray to almost black, and distinctly unlike the usually agreeable, variegated color patterns attained on color case-hardened carbon steel hammers and triggers.

S&W shipped Chiefs Special Model 36 serial number **455586** in November 1966 (Figure 98). It wears a new contoured thumbpiece, and its case-hardened hammer flaunts its colors. The right diamond magna stock has a matching serial number. The first Model 36 I documented with the new contoured thumbpiece came at serial number **404121**.

Figure 98: Chiefs Special Model 36 **455586** with a contoured thumbpiece.

S&W tagged a block of 5,000 serial numbers for a second Model 60 production run. Dr. Jinks' book says law enforcement agencies had objected to the bright polished finish, and "It was difficult for S&W to manufacture" so late in 1966 the company made a change, "polishing the gun to a satin—rather than a bright—finish."

We see a few examples from the second production run with the bright, polished finish, but most documented in the database have the new satin finish. Richard A. Sherburne Incorporated in East Northfield, Massachusetts, placed an order for two Model 60s from Smith & Wesson on November 26, 1965. S&W filled Sherburne's order with Model 60 serial numbers **476024** and **477147** on November 15, 1966, which holds the current record as the second production run's earliest known ship date. Serial number **477147** shows its new satin finish and dark bronze, case-hardened stainless steel hammer and trigger (Figure 99). The gun wears matching-serial number diamond magna stocks.

Figure 99: Second production run Model 60, case-hardened hammer and trigger.

Here's a fun factory flub. It happens. Smith & Wesson shipped this square butt 3" lightweight barrel Chiefs Special Model 36 to American Wholesale Hardware Company in California on May 10, 1967 (Figure 100). Nothing odd yet, right? The serial number stamped on the butt has five digits, "from 1952," the seller said (*right* inset). Uh, no! It looks as though someone used a sharp tool to scratch out the first of six numbers on the otherwise matching-serial number right stock (*center* inset). I do not have the box, but luckily Smith & Wesson still stamped the serial number on the back of the extractor during this era. The last five digits of the poorly stamped serial number—**520386**—on the back of the extractor match the ones on the butt and right stock (*left* inset).

Figure 100 & insets: Chiefs Special Model 36 serial number **520386**.

Smith & Wesson had enjoyed a great relationship with the New York Police Department. When NYPD asked the company to create a 3" Chiefs Special with a heavy barrel, S&W responded. The result gave the new Chiefs Special a new model number. In his book Dr. Jinks clearly explains, "The variation of the Model 36 signified by the -1 is the model designation for the 3" heavy barrel and not an engineering change as on other models." S&W concurrently made the Model 36-1 with a 3" heavy barrel and a Model 36 with either a 2" or 3" lightweight barrel until 1976 when it discontinued the Model 36 3" lightweight barrel (Figure 101).

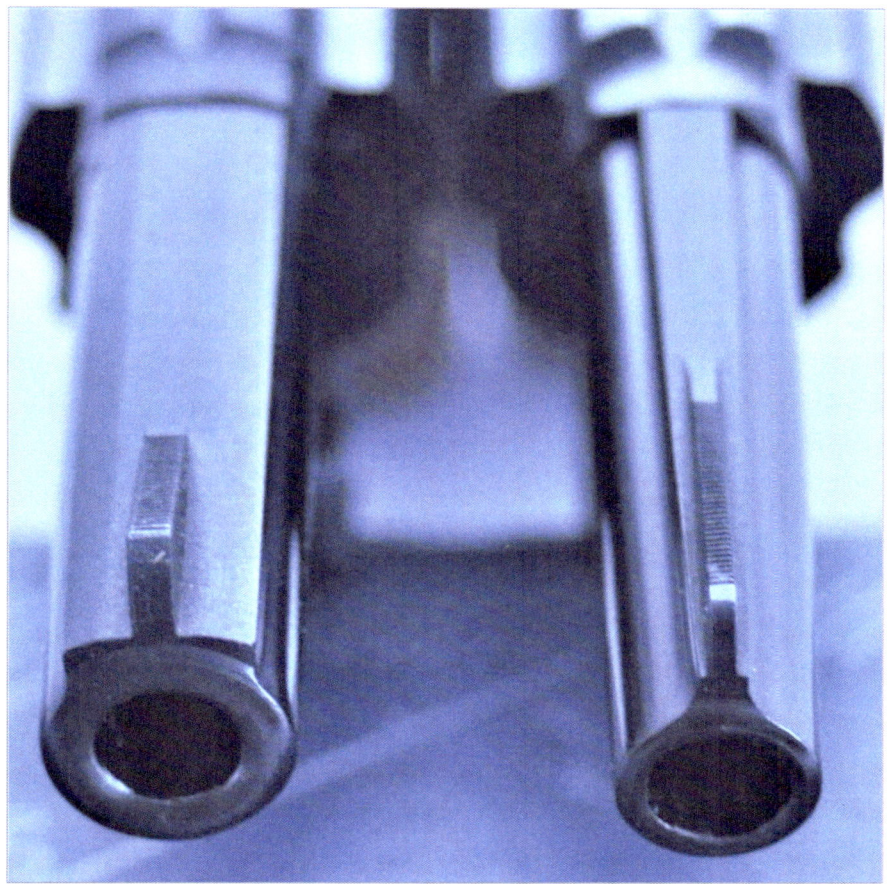

Figure 101: *Left:* Model 36-1 3" heavy barrel, and *right:* Model 36 3" lightweight barrel.

Model 36-1 came with a blue or nickel finish and round or square butt. The heavy barrel's stubby .118" wide front sight seems significant compared to the 3" lightweight barrel's long, $\frac{1}{10}$" (.1") wide front sight.

The first three known 3" Heavy Barrel Chiefs Special Model 36-1s shipped in September 1966, including serial number **456212** to the United States Army's Post Exchange at Fort Belvoir, Virginia. A Smith & Wesson Collectors Association friend bought it at the PX the next month, carried it in Vietnam, and still owns it. S&W shipped Model 36-1 serial number **458157** to Riley's Incorporated in Avilla, Indiana, on July 28, 1967 (Figure 102). Its square butt right diamond magna stock's serial number matches.

Figure 102: 3" Heavy Barrel Chiefs Special Model 36-1 serial number **458157**.

S&W shipped 3" Heavy Barrel Chiefs Special Model 36-1 serial number **466658** to International Distributors Incorporated in Miami, Florida, on September 18, 1967—the United States Air Force's twentieth birthday (Figure 103).

Figure 103: Model 36-1 **466658**. Right stock shows **461658**. Another factory flub?

Smith & Wesson shipped Model 60 serial number **478661** to Evaluators Limited in Quantico, Virginia, on January 26, 1968 (Figure 104). The box top includes *of Bangor Punta* script ahead of the corporate brand (*top* inset). In what appears to be a pivotal, proving-ground second production run, Dr. Jinks explained a new process involved heat treating then flash chroming the stainless steel hammers and triggers. This gun's hammer and trigger show the result. The appearance seems to agree with the new satin finish, which the revised product brochure reflects (*bottom* inset). The serial number on the right diamond magna stock matches the butt and the box, which wears the Carpenter Steel Company logo.

Figure 104 & insets: Second production run Model 60, flash chromed hammer & trigger.

S&W blocked a set of 1,503 serial numbers for the third Model 60 production run. Stories say production did not meet demand. S&W had solved problems and set standards, though, and the satin finish and flash chromed hammers and triggers would carry on for nearly three decades.

Did inflation caused by the Vietnam War force S&W to raise its Model 60 price? After two years at $90 the price jumped to $100 effective March 1, 1968. S&W shipped Model 60 serial number **490035** to Warner Hardware Company in Minneapolis, Minnesota, on March 22, 1968 (Figure 105). The Warner Hardware Company receipt dated April 15, 1968, shows the $100 sale price. Please note the traditional ampersand in the text on the left side of the barrel (inset).

Figure 105: Serial numbers match on the box, butt, right stock, and sales receipt of this third production run Model 60 **490035**. Inset: Traditional ampersand on the barrel.

Chiefs Special model lineups continued without change into 1968, except some diamond magna stock inventory must have been depleted. Shipped in April 1968, 3" lightweight barrel Chiefs Special Model 36 serial number **597497** wears square butt matching-serial number magna stocks sans diamonds (Figure 106).

Figure 106: 3" Chiefs Special Model 36 **597497** with magna stocks sans diamonds.

S&W blocked 4,000 and 6,550 numbers for Model 60 production runs four and five, hinting S&W had heeded the call for more stainless Chiefs Specials. From the fifth production run Smith & Wesson shipped Model 60 serial number **621079** on August 29, 1968, to Williams Gun Sight Company in Davison, Michigan (Figure 107). This year we also see alloy, carbon steel, and stainless steel round butt Chiefs Specials wearing magna stocks with recessed escutcheons and no diamonds. The stocks' checking pattern and shape come close to matching the previous stocks with diamonds. The boxes have the *of Bangor Punta* script and a variant Carpenter Steel Company logo (inset). Examples shipped earlier in the run bear the original Carpenter Steel Company logo.

Figure 107: Fifth production run Model 60 **621079** wears magna stocks sans diamonds. Inset: Variant Carpenter Steel Company logo with "made to serve you better" text.

Figure 108: Fourth production run Model 60 **515970**. Inset: Text on box top.

The Model 60's fourth production run serial number **515970** shipped on January 29, 1969, to Belknap Hardware and Manufacturing Company in Louisville, Kentucky (Figure 108). Its matching-serial number box does not have a Carpenter Steel Company logo, and its top includes a familiar line we see into the 1980s: a brand followed by A BANGOR PUNTA COMPANY in all capital letters with varying font sizes (inset). This Model 60 has serial number-matching diamond magna stocks. February 1969 marks the last known ship date for a Model 60 with serial number-matching diamond magna stocks, serial number **515829**, which belongs to Smith & Wesson Collectors Association friend Joe Cebull.

Smith & Wesson shipped Chiefs Special Airweight Model 37 serial number **707084** to the United States Navy's Naval Surface Warfare Center in Crane, Indiana, on March 5, 1969 (Figure 109). S&W stamped the serial number in the frame's yoke cut because it put a lanyard ring through the butt's serial number (inset). Smith & Wesson Collectors Association friend and military arms guru Kevin Williams told me the United States Navy tests equipment for its sea, air, and land teams (SEALs) at its Crane, Indiana, facility.

Figure 109 & inset: Chiefs Special Airweight Model 37 **707084** with lanyard ring.

Instead of assembling Model 37s without a serial number on the butt to fill the Navy order, did Smith & Wesson simply take models from the vault, stamp the serial number on the frames, drill the holes through the serial numbers on the butts, and then install lanyard rings? Details on this order are incomplete so we may never find an answer.

My database lists twenty-five in the order in serial range 707028-707284, and three outliers with lanyard rings but not in this shipment: serial number **531697** went to the Naval Surface Warfare Center on the same date, March 5, 1969; serial number **703696** with an unknown ship date or destination; and serial number **709985** shipped in June 1970 to an unknown destination.

Matching-serial number magna stocks are a new style with the shorter, narrower checking area, and new perimeter design, a shape we see with slight variations into the 1990s.

S&W blocked 3,000 and 250 numbers for the last two Model 60 production runs with serial numbers in the original J-frame series. I have documented several from the sixth production run with original boxes, but only one, shipped in October 1968, had a Carpenter Steel Company logo, the variant. Known examples have new magna stocks with a smaller checking area. S&W shipped sixth production run serial number **655768** on July 13, 1969, to Amarillo Hardware Company in Amarillo, Texas.

Smith & Wesson sent ten Model 60s to Jesse Harpe Company in Tampa Bay, Florida, on May 12, 1969, the seventh production run's sole known ship date. The order includes serial number **712089**.

Serial number **761437** is the first known blue 3" Chiefs Special to have an ampersand in the Smith & Wesson text on the barrel's left side to appear like this: **&**. Model 36 serial number **786544** is the highest serial number in the original Chiefs Special serial number series.

- -

Wouldn't I like to find these Chiefs Specials from this era?

1) Model 60 from the sixth production run

3) Model 60 from the seventh production run

Keep your revolver near you night and day,
   And never relax your precautions.
      —Arther Conan Doyle

Chapter 6

1969-1983

.38 Chiefs Special
    J serials: Models 36, 36-1, 37, & 50
    R serials: Models 60 & 60-1

Responding to Gun Control Act of 1968 requirements, S&W assigned letter J to four consecutive serial number series for alloy and carbon steel Bodyguard and Chiefs models. S&W used the letter R for stainless Model 60 serial numbers R1-R332516, and shipped the first one, serial number **R93**, on May 23, 1969. Smith & Wesson also used the R prefix for .38 Terrier Model 32-1 and .38 Regulation Police Model 33-1, both discontinued in 1974; a limited production square butt 3" Heavy Barrel Model 60-1 in 1972; and the new stainless Model 651 in 1982.

Other J-frame models used letters H, L, and M. Writing about "serial number systems" in the late 1970s, Dr. Jinks said, "The J-frame model system is probably one of the most complex."

S&W used numeric equipment to stamp serial numbers on the inside of the right stocks so those serial numbers do not include letters.

Figure 110: Model 60 serial number **R3049**. Insets: *Left*, matching-serial number butt and stock, and *right*, the anomaly S stamp on the trigger.

Chiefs Special Model 60 serial number **R3049** shipped to Simon Atlas & Sons Incorporated in Washington, D.C., on July 16, 1969, the day NASA launched the Apollo 11 mission from Kennedy Space Center to put the first man on the moon (Figure 110). The right magna stock's serial number matches the butt's (inset). An anomaly S is stamped on the trigger's upper right side (inset).

S&W's October 1, 1969, catalog listed Model 60 for $110. Model 36s cost $84-blue, $92-nickel; Model 37s cost $86.50-blue, $94.50-nickel; and the catalog did not list Model 36-1.

Smith & Wesson used the first J serial number series with a J plus one to five numbers for Chiefs Special Models 36, 36-1, and 37 through the spring of 1970. S&W shipped Model 36 serial numbers **J145**, owned by my friend Jim DeMarco, and **J9902** in February 1969, the series' earliest known ship date. S&W shipped the last serial number in the series, **J99999**, to J. L. Galef & Son Incorporated in New York City on January 12, 1970, and the first in the series, **J1**, to Smith & Wesson's Southern representative Patterson & Hanson Company in Largo, Florida, on May 1, 1970.

S&W shipped 3" lightweight barrel Chiefs Special Model 36 serial number **J53346** to Barker-Chadsey Company in Johnston, Rhode Island, on March 4, 1970 (Figure 111). Ampersands in the S&W name on some 3" Chiefs' barrels in this series resembled this: **&c** (inset).

Figure 111: 3" Chiefs Special Model 36 **J53346**. Inset: **&c** ampersand in the text on the left side of the barrel.

Smith & Wesson shipped Chiefs Special Model 36 serial number **J75846** to John J. Tobler Sporting Goods Incorporated in Union City, New Jersey, on March 27, 1970 (Figure 112).

Figure 112: Model 36 serial number **J75846**.

Dr. Jinks told me Smith & Wesson's serial number equipment was limited to stamping a maximum of six characters on a J-frame's small butt. The limitation doubtless spurred the next J serial series. Dr. Jinks calls this clever series for Bodyguard models and Chiefs Special Models 36, 36-1, 37, and 50 the "roving J series." He said the series began at **1J1** in 1970. Sandwiched amid two to five digits, one to three before it and one to four after it, the J made its methodical march to the right. Serial number **1J9999** preceded **2J1**, **9J9999** preceded **10J1**, **99J999** preceded **100J1**, and so on up to serial number **999J99** in 1973. Smith & Wesson shipped serial number **1J123**—the first known roving J serial number, a blue 2" Model 36—on April 16, 1970, the first known roving J series ship date, to Richard Sherburne Company in Greenfield, Massachusetts.

Figure 113: Chiefs Special Model 36 serial number **2J4177**.

Chiefs Special Model 36 serial number **2J4177** shipped to Leslie Edelman Incorporated, Southampton, Pennsylvania, on May 29, 1970, my high school graduation day (Figure 113).

S&W shipped Chiefs Special Model 36 serial number **41J619** to Clearfield Hardware Company in Clearfield, Pennsylvania, on May 14, 1971 (Figure 114). Special features include engraved New South Wales Police Force insignia, Bodyguard hammer, and target trigger. Dr. Jinks' letter says, "The invoice does not list any special features, however it is in the middle of a group of 60 revolvers specifically manufactured for the New South Wales Police Department of Australia. It is my opinion that this revolver was accidentally shipped to a domestic distributor by mistake." NSWPF translates its *Latin* motto "*culpam poena premit comes*" on the logo to English as: "Punishment swiftly follows crime" (inset).[13 & 14]

Figure 114: NSWPF Model 36 **41J619**. The target trigger and Bodyguard (Model 49) hammer may or might not be factory original. Inset: NSWPF logo.

A *Smith & Wesson Forum* member said he served "in the New South Wales Police Force for 21 years," and he'd "Seen a few … issued to Detectives and Female Police Officers … but never seen one with a Target Trigger and Model 49 Hammer." He also added, "Apart from a few left over in the Armoury and a couple in museums, they were all destroyed." He inspired me to dig deeper.

In short order I found the website for the Sydney, New South Wales, Justice & Police Museum.[15] The site showed a photo of display #44 with the caption: ".38 CALIBRE SMITH & WESSON REVOLVER (5 shot) for policewomen 1970s." The museum's Model 36 appeared identical to mine, except it had a standard Model 36 hammer and trigger. The last time I searched the updated site I could not locate display #44's photo. So it goes when entities revise their presence on the world stage.

Smith & Wesson shipped Chiefs Special Model 60 serial number **R56729** in December 1971 (Figure 115). The serial number inside the right stock matches. There's nothing flashy or contrary here–simply a nice example of the marque.

Figure 115: Chiefs Special Model 60 serial number **R56729**. Serial numbers inside the right magna stock and on the butt match.

Roving J math: sets of serial numbers with a single digit before the J (i.e., 1-9) produced 9,999 revolvers, sets with two digits before the J (i.e., 10-99) produced 999, and sets with three digits before the J (i.e., 100-999) produced 99. My attempt at math suggests if Smith & Wesson had used every serial number, production could approach 260,000 units.

Model 36 serial number **84J974** shipped the month and year I enlisted in the United States Air Force: March 1972 (Figure 116). Its right stock has a matching serial number.

Figure 116: Chiefs Special Model 36 serial number **84J974**.

Dr. Jinks told me Smith & Wesson obtained new equipment in 1972 capable of stamping seven characters on a J-frame. He sent a Smith & Wesson internal Memorandum from July 1972 that said, "Revolvers [list of internal factory codes for Bodyguards and Chiefs] which have a 'J' and five numbers will end with 999J99 and continue with J100000." Models with R prefix serial numbers carried on without mention because the series had not yet neared the old equipment's max of **R99999**.

Figure 117: Chiefs Special Target Model 50 serial number **935J93**.

On March 11, 1955, Smith & Wesson introduced its 2" Chiefs Special Target model. Dr. Jinks' book said by 1966 S&W had produced 1,543 Chiefs Special Target and Model 36 Target models. In a historical letter for a Model 50 Dr. Jinks said the company had assigned Model 50 in 1962 to separate adjustable target sight parts from fixed sight Model 36 parts, but the company first used the Chiefs Special Target Model 50 designator in 1973 when it set aside 568 serial numbers for the model. Dr. Jinks' recent records search revealed twenty-eight are "Open on the books, did not ship." Smith & Wesson Collectors Association friend Joe Cebull—Chiefs Special Target model expert and curator of the target database—tracks and documents known Chiefs Special Target models. Model 50 serial number **935J93** shipped to B. E. Hodgdon Incorporated in Shawnee Mission, Kansas, on March 27, 1973, my first anniversary in the United States Air Force (Figure 117). In an email Dr. Jinks told me "I have not seen a catalog listing for the Model 50," and he added, "This model has always been manufactured on special request."

Chiefs Special Model 36 serial number **999J68** bears the highest known serial number in the roving J series (Figure 118). Smith & Wesson shipped it to Zale Corporation in Texas on April 11, 1973. Dr. Jinks said, "It appears to be a single unit. That could mean the grips are correct."

Figure 118: Chiefs Special Model 36 **999J68** wears smooth presentation stocks.

Model 50 serial number **J160795**—the only known Model 50 sans a roving J series serial number—and six roving J series Model 50s shipped to B. E. Hodgdon on July 27, 1973 (Figure 119). Dr. Jinks' letter said S&W produced 1,132 Model 50 units through 1977. Where are the other 563 Model 50s? The inset shows Model 50 production math.

Model 50 production			
1,132	Total made	564	Not roving J
- 568	Roving J series	- 1	J160795
--------		-----	
564	Remaining	563	Where are they?

Figure 119: Model 50 serial number **J160795**. Inset: Model 50 production math.

Model 36-1 serial number **J218723** is one of 488 S&W shipped to Jonas Arms and Aircraft Company in New York City on June 21, 1974 (Figure 120). The order included Model 36-1 **J199524**, and it's stamped "CAI Import". They are the sole Model 36-1s I've seen with a traditional ampersand on the barrel's left side (*right* inset). Dr. Jinks believes this order primarily served export customers. Between this serial number and **J349996** the stirrup mainspring rod changed from cylindrical to flat (*left* inset).

Figure 120 & insets: Model 36-1 serial number **J218723**.

Smith & Wesson shipped 3" lightweight barrel Chiefs Special Model 36 serial number **J349996** to Dakin Sporting Goods Company in Bangor, Maine, on July 24, 1975 (Figure 121). Known 3" Chiefs Special Models 36, 36-1, and 37 produced and shipped in 1975/76 use the Greek letter *epsilon* Ɛ ampersand in the text on the barrel's left side (inset).

Figure 121: 3" Chiefs Special **J349996**. Inset: *Epsilon* ampersand.

Shipped in October 1975, 3" Heavy Barrel Chiefs Special Target Model 36-1 serial number **2J3333** came from a run of 213 (Figure 122). Dr. Jinks' book said S&W shipped 202. The 3" Heavy Barrel did not fit in with the Model 50 designator. Roving J 3" Chiefs Specials wear either **&** or generic ampersands on the barrel's left side (inset).

Figure 122 & inset: 3" Heavy Barrel Chiefs Special Model 36-1 Target Model **2J3333**.

In 1950 S&W President Hellstrom wrote, "We have unanimously selected the name 'Chiefs Special' for our new revolver," but he didn't file to trademark protect the model's name as he did for Airweight three years later and Highway Patrolman the next year. Did Hellstrom not file to protect the name because it wasn't stamped on the revolver like the other two? Bangor Punta filed to protect "Chiefs Special" on April 10, 1974, reporting "First use as early as March 8, 1951" (Figure 123). United States Patent and Trademark Office records indicate the office initially registered the CHIEFS SPECIAL trademark on February 24, 1976.[16]

United States Patent Office	Reg. No. 1,034,286
	Registered Feb. 24, 1976

TRADEMARK
Principal Register

CHIEFS SPECIAL

Bangor Punta Operations, Inc. (New York corporation)
1 Greenwich Plaza
Greenwich, Conn.

For: FIREARMS—NAMELY, REVOLVERS—in CLASS 13 (U.S. CL. 9).
First use as early as Mar. 8, 1951; in commerce as early as Mar. 8, 1951.
Without waiving its common law rights, applicant claims no registration rights in the word "Special" apart from the mark as shown.

Ser. No. 18,426, filed Apr. 10, 1974.

DAVID C. REIHNER, Examiner

Figure 123: The office's earliest trademark registration record for CHIEFS SPECIAL.

Figure 124: 3" Heavy Barrel Chiefs Special Model 36-1 **7J4619**, O.S.I. stamped on the frame. These are the only banana stocks I have seen offering the illusion of a whale tail at the top. United States Air Force OSI agent friends gave their challenge coins to me.

Special features on 3" Heavy Barrel Chiefs Special Model 36-1 serial number **7J4619** include O.S.I. stamped on the left side of the frame below the cylinder, banana stocks, and a target trigger (Figure 124). The left side of the barrel wears the **&** ampersand.

OSI symbolizes the United States Air Force's Office of Special Investigations. A *Smith & Wesson Forum* member said, "I carried one of those when I first became an OSI agent," and he added, "I remember the banana grips but not the type of trigger." According to Dr. Jinks' letter, "The revolver shipped with banana stocks. There is no mention of the engraving of 'OSI.' However, the serial number places the revolver in the range of the 1,420 units shipped to the United States Air Force in the spring of 1971." Smith & Wesson shipped this only known example to Richard Sherburne Company in Greenfield, Massachusetts, on April 16, 1976. Is it another shipping mistake, or could it be a contract overrun that lingered in the vault for five years?

In 1976 Smith & Wesson discontinued the 3" lightweight barrel on the Model 36. The company shipped serial number **J465944**, the last one known with the 3" lightweight barrel, to Ashland Shooting Supplies Company in Ashland, Ohio, on July 14, 1976.

Figure 125: Among the first stainless steel square butt 3" Heavy Barrel Chiefs Specials, Model 60-1 **R57195**. Parts made in 1972, 169 assembled and shipped in 1978.

S&W produced parts in 1972 for a test group of the Model 60-1, the first stainless Chiefs with 3" Heavy Barrels and square butts. Like Model 36-1, this is not an engineering change but a new model. Dr. Jinks told me, "The parts were not assembled or marketed except for a few experimental test revolvers." Serial number **R57306** shipped to Jonas Arms & Aircraft Company in New York City on May 18, 1972. Rather than scrap the parts, in 1978 Smith & Wesson offered the revolvers to its distributors. Smith & Wesson's Model 60-1 shipping records for serial range R56962-R57243 show the company assembled 169 units, and then shipped them to eight different distributors on June 12, 1978. Records list 113 as "Open on the books, did not ship." Smith & Wesson shipped Model 60-1 serial number **R57195** and twenty others to Gil Hebard Guns Incorporated in Knoxville, Illinois (Figure 125).

In 1977 the United States Navy placed a special order for blue 2" Chiefs Special Model 36s with a "U.S." military property stamp on the back strap and a lanyard ring. Smith & Wesson assigned serial number range J580001–J584580 and shipped 4,278 units to the Navy. The company made more than ordered in case the Navy rejected any. Navy did not. Unlike Navy's 1969 Chiefs Special Airweight Model 37 shipments the company did not stamp serial numbers on the butt before installing the lanyard rings (Figure 126). Like the earlier Navy order, though, Smith & Wesson stamped the serial number on the frame above the model number in the yoke cut (Figure 127).

Figure 126: Lanyard ring in butt.   Figure 127: Serial number on frame.

Shipping records show 225 "Open on the books, did not ship." S&W sold seventy-seven Navy contract overrun units to five different distributors from September 1978 to June 1980. S&W shipped Chiefs Special Model 36 serial number **J581423**, one of nineteen in the order, to AAA Police Supply Company in Dedham, Massachusetts, on June 23, 1980 (Figure 128). Kevin Williams and I recently shared our lists of known overruns, expanding both our lists to a total of twenty-seven. The right stocks on my model and seven others have no serial number, three have a serial number different than the frame, and sixteen we do not know.

Figure 128: Chiefs Special Model 36 **J581423** with lanyard ring, Navy contract overrun.

Gun show pal Thom Braxton once told me, "A cleanup boy had overheard S&W execs pondering how to sell the U.S. marked overruns on the civilian market." Thom said, "The boy made the suggestion to stamp 'MADE IN   A.' over the 'U.S.' property stamp." True? I asked Dr. Jinks, and he said, "Bob, that is a true story." Mired in the thick of it, Smith & Wesson Handgun Product Manager Roy G. Jinks submitted the order for the stamp and solved the problem (Figure 129).

Figure 129: MADE IN U.S.A. stamp on Model 36 **J581423**.

S&W contracted a firm in Italy to engrave some products in this era. S&W shipped Chiefs Special Model 36 serial number **J849971** on the United States Constitution's 194th birthday, September 17, 1981, to John Jovino Company in New York City (Figure 130). It wears smooth rosewood presentation stocks and Class A engraving done by the Italian firm, one of eleven Chiefs of this configuration in the shipment.

Figure 130: Engraved Model 36 **J849971** wearing rosewood presentation stocks.

Within a month of shipping this engraved Model 36 Smith & Wesson shipped engraved Model 60 serial numbers **R267665**, **R275206** and **R275857**. They came configured with the presentation stocks, and the second and third serial numbers' engraving mirrors this Model 36.

S&W increased the logo size on the J-frames' left side in this era. The new larger logo first showed up on Chiefs Special Model 36 serial number **J950585**, shipped to Dave's House of Guns Incorporated in Dallas, Texas, on April 5, 1982.

S&W began developing its Distinguished Magnum L-frame revolvers in 1979. Designed sans a barrel pin, the idea led the company to eliminate barrel pins on all its models. Dr. Jinks told me, "It was the result of changing barrel threads to be a slight mismatch to the frame that locked the barrel firmly in place." Figure 131 shows a Model 36 barrel removed from its frame and turned ninety degrees left of its normal position. The machined slot on top is where the pin rides to align the front sight and lock the barrel into the frame.

Figure 131: Barrel's machined slot for the barrel pin.

Dr. Jinks told me, "The J-frames were the first of the production models to lose the barrel pin." He has a 1980 Smith & Wesson catalog that shows a photo of a Model 36 without the barrel pin. S&W shipped serial number **J962796**—the last known Model 36 in this serial number series that has a barrel pin—to Automatic Distributing Corporation in Batesville, Texas, on May 1, 1982.

Improved production practices meant stocks no longer needed to be hand fitted or numbered. Machining consistency meant any stocks of one size and shape should fit any frame with the same size and shape. Blue 2" square butt Model 36 serial number **J953981** wears the last known serial number-matching stocks.

Although this serial number series ran to serial number **J999999**, Chiefs Special Model 36-1 serial number **J970318** has the last known ship date in the series, February 1983.

The J-frames might have been the first to begin losing their barrel pins, but aluminum alloy and carbon steel Bodyguards and Chiefs Specials were among the last of the models Smith & Wesson transitioned to its new universal serial number series. Instead of making the switch after serial number **J999999**, Smith & Wesson used a brief extension of the roving J series in 1982-83.

Bodyguard and Chiefs models bore serial numbers in the 1J00000–1J47502 range. Blue 2" Model 36 serial number **1J03963** has the earliest known Chiefs Special ship date in this series, August 1982. No known Model 50 is serial numbered in this series. Fewer than a handful of the Chiefs Specials I have documented in the database from this serial series have a barrel pin. All have the new large S&W logo on the left side of the frame below the thumbpiece.

An order for five Chiefs Specials, including nickel 2" Model 36 square butt serial number **1J09990**, shipped on November 24, 1982, to Sports South in Grimes, Iowa.

Most known models in this series shipped by early 1983, but one late shipper, nickel 2" Model 36 serial number **1J02454**, shipped on November 16, 1985, to Abercrombie & Fitch in New York City (Figure 132). It has the new large logo on the frame's left side and no barrel pin.

Figure 132: Nickel Chiefs Special Model 36 **1J02454**. New large logo and nc barrel pin.

Another late shipper, blue 2" Model 37 serial number **1J30660**, shipped on February 27, 1986, to Mile High Sporting Goods Company in Denver, Colorado.

- -

Wouldn't I like to find these Chiefs Specials from this era?

1) The two-tone Model 50 I saw in a Biloxi, Mississippi, gun shop in November 1974

2) Model 60, one of eight sent to Mr. Hoffman at the Consulate of Pakistan in Boston, Massachusetts, on January 2, 1979, custom engraving & *bright blue finish*, serial range R219xxx+. Dr. Jinks told me these are the only Model 60s he's heard of—other than his—with a bright blue finish.

3) Model 60, commemorative for the Missouri Highway Patrol 50th anniversary (1931-81), serial range R326xxx

If you don't like something, change it.
If you can't change it, change your attitude.
— Maya Angelou

Chapter 7

1982-1996

.38 Chiefs Specials
   Alphanumeric serial numbers
   Product Code (PC) numbers
   Engineering change numbers

It is my honor to caretake the Chiefs presented herein and narrate their story. The barn contains a legion of empty stalls. I have filled some vacancies with details of a few models friends own, others I have seen, and examples I have yet to acquire. This, the play's seventh act, posed a particularly perplexing predicament. The period's prodigious audition list overflows with special actors so more vacancies than filled stalls exist. My sage friend John Heckert's wise words whistle in the wind against my will: "You can't own 'em all, Bob."

The new alphanumeric serial numbers began at AAA0001 when Smith & Wesson launched its Distinguished Magnum L-frame revolvers in 1980. Through the next few years the company systematically sifted other models into this new series. Serial usage, certainly not shipping, seems to follow alphabetical then numerical order. I have not seen serial numbers with four zeros, but members of the *Smith & Wesson Forum* said they have so that could mean AAA9999 precedes AAB0000 and so on. Exceptions exist for special or limited production runs of certain models.

Smith & Wesson shipped the Chiefs Special with the first known alphanumeric serial number on March 15, 1983: nickel 2" Model 36 serial number **AAL0963**. Other notable Chiefs include the series' first known ship date, December 1982, a blue 2" Model 36 serial number **AAR5697**. In February 1983 S&W shipped the first known Model 37, serial number **AAM0040**, and the first known Model 60, serial number **AAS2345**, which is the last known Chiefs Special with a narrow, serrated trigger, and it has a barrel pin. Blue 2" square butt Model 36 serial number **AAU2407**, the last known Chiefs Special with a barrel pin, has this era's new standard smooth combat trigger. Serial number **AAM4629** is the first known 3" Heavy Barrel Model 36-1 in this serial series. No known Model 50 bears an alphanumeric serial number.

S&W also added a six-digit, model-specific Product Code or stock-keeping unit (SKU). The company designated PC 101501 to the ubiquitous blue 2" round butt Model 36, PC 101602 to a blue 2" round butt Model 37, and PC 102302 to Model 60.

S&W made the only known run of 600 stainless square butt 2" Chiefs Special Model 60s for John Jovino Company in New York City. Dr. Jinks calls them "the Jovino Special." S&W shipped serial number **AEC3787** to Jovino in June 1984 (Figure 133). PC 102303.

Figure 133: Square butt 2" Model 60 **AEC3787**, a Jovino exclusive.

Jovino's success with the 2" model inspired the company to order 1,000 stainless 3" Chiefs Specials with square butts. S&W shipped 3" Heavy Barrel Model 60 serial number **AEV5542** to Jovino in December 1984 (Figure 134). PC 102304. This limited run created the first and only known 3" Heavy Barrel Chiefs Specials sans -1 model number. Did this omen warn us not to expect future stainless Chiefs model numbers to march in lockstep with their Airweight and carbon steel brethren? Lear Siegler Incorporated bought Bangor Punta Corporation in January 1984. Did Lear Siegler turn a blind eye to historic precedent?

Figure 134: Square butt 3" Heavy Barrel Model 60 **AEV5542**.

	SMITH & WESSON			.38 caliber
J06				
Model No.	Barrel	Fin.	Stock	Features
60	3	S	SB	
Serial No.	Product Code			Spec. Ord.	Pkr.
AEV5542	102304		X	4226
AEV5542	0600093031		X	A18-3616

Figure 135: Label.

New labels on new boxes show a model number, the barrel length, type finish, stock (square butt), serial number, PC, and Spec. Ord. (the gun's packing date?) as a Julian date—year then day: 4226 = 1984, August 13 (Figure 135).

The Virginia State Police Auxiliary ordered 370 Chiefs Special Model 60s well in advance to celebrate the VSP's fifty-fifth Anniversary. S&W shipped serial number **AFP6021** to Tidewater Police Supply and Sporting Goods Company in New Port News, Virginia, on May 30, 1985 (Figure 136). PC 102302. Ken Hurst of Rustburg, Virginia, engraved side plates with patches worn by Virginia Troopers in 1932 and 1987, script-engraved back straps *V.S.P. 55th Anniversary Ed.* (*left* inset), and engraved 180 with a scroll pattern flaunting an agreeable elegance absent on the stageful of other law enforcement commemoratives. The scroll-engraved Model 60 nestles in the blue velvet interior of its oak presentation case with an etched VSP Trooper badge centered on the lid (*right* inset). I've seen several of the 190 non-scroll-engraved Model 60s in their wooden cases with wood-framed, etched-glass lids.

Figure 136 & insets: Virginia State Police 55th Anniversary Edition Model 60 **AFP6021**.

S&W's first Model 60-1, the 1972 square butt 3" Heavy Barrel, followed the model numbering precedent set in 1966 by the 3" Heavy Barrel Model 36-1. S&W's Jovino square butt 3" Heavy Barrel Model 60 jumped the tracks, and the 2" Chiefs Special Target Model 60-1 veered further off course. PC 102305.

Stories say Smith & Wesson made up to 1,000 2" Model 60-1s in 1985 for Ashland Shooting Supplies Company in Ashland, Ohio. Known prefixes include AIV, ALA, ALU, and ANB. Dr. Jinks said, "There are only six serial numbers listed as AIV, and these revolvers were returned to S&W in August 1991 and reshipped to dealers who returned them in October 1991. My thoughts on this are that ATF did not want S&W to use a capital I in the serial numbers as it could be mistaken for a 1." My database lists nine AIV Model 60-1s Dr. Jinks did not find in the records. He said, "ALU0697-ALU2224 [1,528] are Model 60-1s," and he added "ALU3160-ALU4399 produced 1,240, and ... starts again at ALU4490-ALU5576 [1,087]. ANB4963-ANB5484 [522] are Ashland Model 60-1s." These 4,377 numbers plus up to 600 in range ALU68xx-ALU73xx in my database approach the 5,000 Ashland listed in its advertisement in *The Shotgun Times* on July 10, 1986. John Heckert shared the ad with me.

On September 20, 1814, six days after he wrote his famous poem, "Defense of Fort McHenry," Francis Scott Key published it as a song, "The Star Spangled Banner." Smith & Wesson shipped Model 60-1 **ALU1683** to Ashland the same day 171 years later in 1985 (Figure 137). We also commemorated the sixth annual POW/MIA Recognition Day that day. The sole known ALA Model 60-1, **ALA6921**, was in the shipment.

Figure 137: Chiefs Special Target Model 60-1 **ALU1683** shipped September 20, 1985.

Peru's government ordered 250 Chiefs Special Airweight Model 37s for its version of the U.S. Federal Bureau of Investigation in 1981. I told Dr. Jinks, "Tall tales tell of S&W dispatching two agents to Peru to retrieve the guns for nonpayment." He replied, "My guess knowing S&W, who always wants pay in advance, forced the Peruvian Government to cancel the order." Text stamped around a logo on the side plate of Model 37 serial number **ACE6741** says, *Policia de Investigaciones del Peru* (Figure 138). One of twenty-four in the shipment, Smith & Wesson shipped this Model 37 to Go Wholesale in Billings, Montana, on February 27, 1986. (Figure 139 & inset). PC 101601.

Smith & Wesson placed ads in gun periodicals in 1984 that announced due to Peru's government reorganization, 1,984 Model 10s and 250 Model 37s with the Peruvian police logo would be available through its distributors.

Figure 138:
Policia de Investigaciones del Peru text
around the logo on the Model 37 side plate.

Figure 139 & inset: Peruvian marked Chiefs Special Airweight Model 37 **ACE6741**.

British holding company R. L. Tompkins P.L.C. bought Smith & Wesson in 1987. The 2" Chiefs Special Model 36-2, first engineering change number for a carbon steel Chiefs Special, replaced Model 36 in 1988. Lew Horton Distributing Company's Earl Minot said in his letter serial number **BBT5174** is an early example of S&W's laser etching, one of 502, and S&W shipped it to Horton in April 1989 (Figures 140 & 141). PC 101501. Minot included Horton's ad showing this Model 36 as a "Freedom" Design second amendment Horton Exclusive (Figure 142).

Figure 140: Model 36-2 serial number **BBT5174**.

Figure 141: Etching on side plate. Figure 142: Horton's ad. (Courtesy of Earl Minot)

Chiefs Special 3" Heavy Barrel Model 36-3 Lady Smith serial number **BDN8895** shipped in April 1989 sporting special Goncalo Alves stocks Smith & Wesson reportedly had designed to fit women's hands (Figure 143). The only models I've seen with these stocks are 3" Heavy Barrel Lady Smith Models 36-3, 60-3, and 60-7. I have not seen Models 36-4, 36-5, or 60-6 so I do not know which stocks they wear. The 3" Heavy Barrel Model 36-3 replaced the 3" Heavy Barrel Model 36-1. S&W used hard plastic burgundy cases for its 2" and 3" Lady Smiths through 1991 (inset).

Figure 143 & inset: 3" Heavy Barrel Model 36-3 Lady Smith **BDN8895**. PC 101517.

Figure 144: 3" Heavy Barrel Stainless Model 60-3 Lady Smith **BDV5668**. PC 102309.

Chiefs Special 3" Heavy Barrel Model 60-3 Lady Smith serial number **BDV5668** also shipped in April 1989 (Figure 144). I have put these Lady Smiths in many a Wyomingites' hand at shows across the Cowboy State. As for the stocks ladies declare, "They're the best, *ev •er.*" S&W filed for a Lady Smith trademark on May 18, 1989, and the United States Patent and Trademark Office registered it on January 23, 1990.

S&W made four special runs of Double Action Only Chiefs in 1989. Smith & Wesson shipped Model 36-2 serial numbers **BDW2341** in April and **BDW2435** in May (Figure 145). Both have the smoothest Chiefs Special double action triggers I've felt. They wear a finish called "blue—glass bead-blasted" and handsome S&W Goncalo Alves Combat stocks, which gents seem to like. The three other DAO Chiefs include a blue 3" Model 36-3 and stainless 2" and 3" Model 60-3s.

Figure 145: Double Action Only Model 36-2s with factory bobbed hammers, combat stocks, combat triggers, and a blue—glass bead-blasted finish. PC 101520.

In addition to the DAO Chiefs Smith & Wesson's January 1990 Special Products Bulletin lists twenty-one other 1989 special releases. PC 102316 defines a Chiefs Special Model 60 with an unfluted cylinder. PC 101549's New Product Information sheet names it a "Model 36 with 3" Full Lug Barrel, Adjustable Rear Sight," and calls its finish "blue—glass bead-blasted." Model 36-6 serial number **BEA8859** shipped in July 1989

(Figure 146). Its ribbed barrel with a full lug was a first for a Chiefs Special Target model (inset). Hogue, the original equipment manufacturer (OEM), supplied the model's Monogrip. Dr. Jinks' history letters said it is one of "2,000 target models in this configuration."

Figure 146: 3" Chiefs Special Target Model 36-6 **BEA8859**. Inset: Ribbed barrel

Figure 147: NYPD Model 60-2 NY-1 **BAA6630**. Inset: Frame stamps.

NYPD ordered a DAO stainless Chiefs Special in 1987. S&W made the Chiefs Special Models 60 then NYPD-exclusive 60-2 (1988)

DAO with a bobbed hammer and stamped NY-1 on the frame in the yoke cut. PC 102308. S&W shipped 4,000 units to NYPD's Equipment Bureau for resale to NYPD officers. NYPD soon declared the models unserviceable. The department's armorers made a repair, stamped the repaired models with a silhouette target near the NY-1, and returned those models to the officers. Initially NYPD approved returning the revolvers to service but soon took them out of service for good. Great thanks to Smith & Wesson Collectors Association friend and noted NYPD Historian R. M. Vivas for sharing these NY-1 details in an email. NYPD's Equipment Bureau didn't sell Model 60-2 NY-1 serial number **BAA6630** to an officer (Figure 147 & inset). Robert said, "It is one of 1,232 NYPD returned to S&W." S&W converted it to original Model 60 configuration and shipped it to another distributor in October 1989.

Smith & Wesson shipped Chiefs Special Model 36-7 Lady Smith serial number **BKP9865** in October 1991 (Figure 148). Both carbon steel and stainless steel Lady Smith models with 2" barrels wear the smooth laminated rosewood presentation stocks. For thirty-nine years 2" Chiefs Specials wore a standard ⅒" wide ramp front sight (inset *left*). A Model 36-7 engineering change widened the front sight to a far more visible ⅛" (inset *right*).

Figure 148: Model 36-7 Lady Smith **BKP9865**. Inset: ⅒" & ⅛" sight widths.

Similar to Model 36-6, 3" full lug barrel Chiefs Special Target Model 60-4 has a ribbed barrel and adjustable sights. The target hammer is an upgrade, and unlike this era's other Chiefs it has a serrated combat trigger. I've documented Model 60-4s shipped between 1990 and 1996. The first known Model 60-4 serial number begins BBK; the last known begins CAU. Serial number **BND1101** shipped in August 1992 (Figure 149). Uncle Mike's modeled its OEM combat grips after renowned grip maker Craig Spegel's design. PC 102298.

Figure 149: 3" full lug barrel Chiefs Special Target Model 60-4 **BND1101**.

Dr. Jinks told me stainless 3" Chiefs Special Target Model 60-7 has adjustable sights and a full lug ribbed barrel. He said, "Serial range BFY6285-BFY6808 is 524 units, and they appear to have shipped to domestic distributors. The SKU is 102298." I have not seen one. I imagine one of these would be a coveted find.

Smith & Wesson shipped Chiefs Special Model 60-7 Lady Smith serial number **BPE9507** in October 1993 in a burgundy cloth case Bob Allen made for S&W (Figure 150). PC 102290. Like other known 2" Chiefs Special Lady Smith models it has laminated rosewood stocks. Smith & Wesson's 2005 Engineering Change list said the Model 60-7's front sight widened to ⅛", and a heat treatment strengthened the stainless steel.

Figure 150: Chiefs Special Model 60-7 Lady Smith **BPE9507** on its Bob Allen case.

Figure 151 & insets: Performance Center 3" Model 60 ET Comp **PCQ0108**. PC 170029.

S&W's touted Performance Center conjured up its first Chiefs Special in a limited edition run of 325 units for Lew Horton Distributing Company. Performance Center calls the Model 60-7 a Model 60 ET Comp. S&W's internal code E identifies a J-frame, and T denotes target for a typical non-target model. Performance Center calls its kindred K-frame the Model 66 F Comp. Model 66 is a target model so adding a T to its name would be superfluous. A Performance Center logo replaced the

S&W logo on the frame. Performance Center model serial numbers start with **PC** and use the next alphabetical letter for each subsequent model. Dr. Jinks told me 144 of the Performance Center Chiefs begin PCQ and 181 begin PCR. Dr. Jinks also said serial number **PCR0180** shipped to Rattana Firearms L. P. in Bangkok, Thailand, and the company shipped serial number **PCQ0108** to Horton in October 1993 (Figure 151). The beveled 3" full lug ribbed barrel has an oval compensator atop the barrel ahead of the dovetailed target front sight (*left* inset). A smooth combat trigger interacts with the target hammer. OEM Badger Custom Grips' smooth laminated rosewoods are the company's "3-finger combat-style." The right grip sports an inlaid mother-of-pearl diamond (*right* inset).

I've seen six examples of 3" Heavy Barrel Chiefs Special Model 36-8. Like Model 36-7, the front sight width grew to ⅛". Model 36-8, the twentieth century's last 3" carbon steel Chiefs Special, has the last hammer-mounted firing pin. Uncle Mike's also modeled its OEM boot grips after Craig Spegel's design. S&W shipped serial number **BRY8828** in August 1994, my last month in United States Air Force enlisted grade E-8 (Figure 152). Challenge coins came from Kunsan Air Base, Republic of Korea, where I served when I sewed on the service's top enlisted rank: Chief Master Sergeant.

Figure 152: 3" Heavy Barrel Chiefs Special Model 36-8 **BRY8828**. PC 101510.

Figure 153 shows another 3" full lug barrel Chiefs Special Target Model 60-4. Smith & Wesson shipped serial number **BSP8216** in March

1995. Target hammers and serrated combat triggers on later Model 60-4s, including serial numbers **BRN4673** and after, do not have the old standard flash chromed finish.

Figure 153: 3" full lug barrel Chiefs Special Target Model 60-4 **BSP8216**.

- -

Postscript: My August 2025 review of Smith & Wesson catalogs available in "Resources" on the Smith & Wesson Collectors Association website revealed 1988 was the last catalog available on the site where the company, under the ownership of R. L. Tompkins P.L.C., used the name Chiefs Special to identify a blue carbon steel Model 36. Several models composed of alternative materials, including a stainless steel Model 60, retained the name in the 2000 catalog, but it was the last catalog to note the trademarked name. Stubbornness, respect, precedent, and nostalgia force me to continue using the Chiefs Special name with model numbers.

- -

Wouldn't I like to discover all these missing characters from this era's Chiefs Special audition list?

1) Model 60, Four Queens Casino ~1983

2) 2" Model 60, Kentucky State Police ~1984

3) 2" Model 60, Virginia State Police 55th Anniversary, not scroll engraved, etched trooper badge on the glass lid, 1 of 190, AFP, AFS, & AFV serial ranges, 1985

4) 2" Model 36, 100th anniversary of Massachusetts Chiefs of Police, etched logo on the side plate and wood case's glass lid, 1 of 100, ANS serial range, 1987

5) Model 60, Louisville Police

6) Model 60, Saudi Arabian crest

7) 2" Model 60-3, Michigan State Police, unfluted cylinder, 1989

8) 2" Model 36-2

9) 3" Model 36-3

10) 3" Model 36-3 square butt (last known square butt Chiefs Special)

11) 2" Model 37-1

12) 2" Model 60, NY-1, DAO, AWP serial range, silhouette stamp above NY-1 on frame

13) 2" Model 36-2 Lady Smith

14) 2" Model 60-3 Lady Smith

15) 3" DAO Model 36-3

16) 2" DAO Model 60-3

17) 3" DAO Model 60-3

18) Model 36-4 Lady Smith

19) Model 36-5 Lady Smith

20) Model 60-5 NYPD exclusive

21) Model 60-6 Lady Smith

22) 2" Model 37-2, $\frac{1}{8}$" front sight width

23) 3" Model 60-7 Lady Smith

24) 3" Model 60-7 Target

25) Model 60-8 NYPD exclusive

Every sequel needs to be bigger and better.
—Jason Statham

Chapter 8

1996-2024

Chiefs Specials
    J-Magnum Frame
    Internal Lock

Smith & Wesson made stagy J-frame changes in 1996, notably its J-Magnum frame. Cylinders and frames grew longer to accommodate the .357 Magnum cartridge. The added frame length appears in front of the trigger guard, which remained the same size as the 1952 design for the four-screw Chiefs Special Airweight. S&W milled in a brawny new integral frame lug to replace the long-standard riveted-in part. Production efficiencies prompted a change to manufacture metal injection molded (MIM) triggers, beveled thumbpieces, and flat-faced hammers that strike frame-mounted firing pins.

Smith & Wesson introduced its J-Magnum frame but continued to offer Chiefs Specials in .38 S&W Special. A reason eludes me. Might the .38 S&W Special better serve export markets? Chiefs Special Model 36-9 shows J-Magnum external features, but true to Chiefs heritage its chambers hold .38 S&W Special cartridges. Model 36-9 serial number **CCN7472**, one of eight I have documented, sports Uncle Mike's boot grips. S&W shipped it in February 1998 (Figure 154). PC 101502. Model 36-9 Lady Smiths I have seen wear OEM Altamont laminated rosewood boot stocks without Smith & Wesson medallions.

Figure 154: Chiefs Special Model 36-9 **CCN7472**, J-Magnum frame.

Chambered in .357 Magnum, J-Magnum frame 3" full lug barrel Chiefs Special Target Model 60-10 serial number **CCR8573** shipped to Lew Horton Distributing Company on April 16, 1998 (Figure 155). PC 102430. Dr. Jinks told me, "It was one of 94 in serial range CCR8504-CCR8597 shipped in April to various distributors." It wears Uncle Mike's combat grips. Smith & Wesson made two stainless steel .357 Magnum models, 60-9 and 60-10, followed by three distinct J-Magnum framed Model 60s chambered in .38 S&W Special.

Figure 155: 3" full lug barrel Target Model 60-10 **CCR8573**, .357 Magnum.

The sole known Model 60-11 is serial number **CBU6266**. It has a 2⅛" full lug barrel and OEM Uncle Mike's combat grips (Figure 156 and inset). PC 102438. Dr. Jinks said it shipped as a single unit to Lew Horton on December 9, 1998. He added, "The serial range I found for this group is CBU6259-CBU6342. Most of them shipped to Full Metal SA in Buenos Aires, Argentina, and Baja Firearms in Bangkok, Thailand."

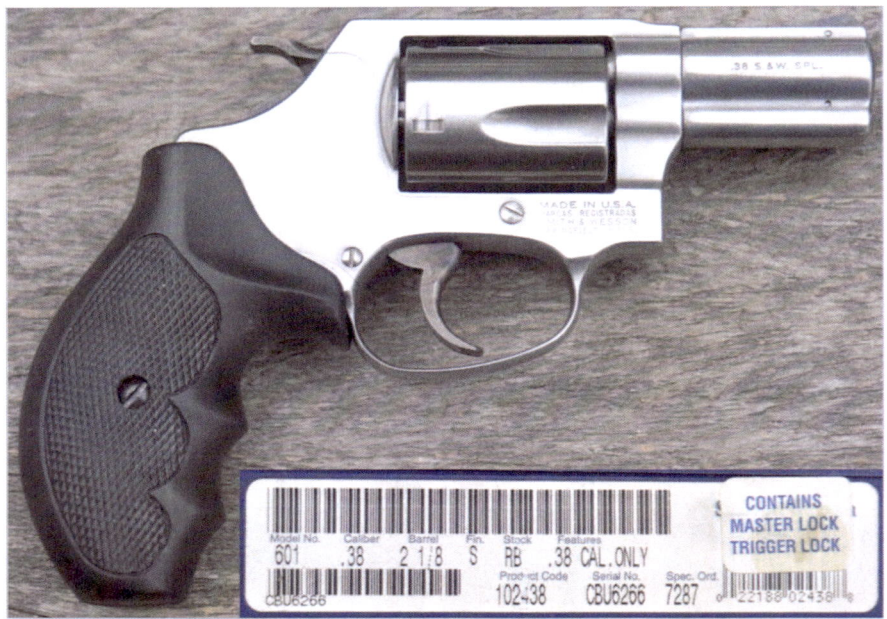

Figure 156: Chiefs Special Model 60-11 **CBU6266**. This is the only one of this model known in the United States. Are there others? Inset: Box end label.

The 2" Model 60-12 has SMITH & WESSON stamped above 38 S.&W. SPL on the left side of its 2" barrel, and for the first time in Chiefs Special history the right side does not offer any information. PC 102423. I've documented four 2" Model 60-12s with CCE, CCM, CCP, and CCS serial prefixes. I am fascinated by the J-Magnum frames offered in .38 S&W Special caliber, but I have not found one of these to wrangle into the herd. Dr. Jinks said serial range CCM4464-CCM4554 sold in February 1998 to Two Brothers Firearms Company in Bangkok, Thailand, but a *Smith & Wesson Forum* member said he bought serial number **CCM4547** in the United States in August 1998. Another forum member said his Model 60-12 is a 3" full lug barrel target model, which S&W's 2005 Engineering Change list does not report.

I've seen four stainless 3" full lug barrel Chiefs Special Target Model 60-13s. Dr. Jinks told me, "Serial numbers CCB5429-CCB5618 shipped on September 2, 1997, to Yothin Firearm L. P. in Bangkok, Thailand. I have noted one of these returned and sold to an American Distributor." S&W shipped serial number **CCB4700** on December 22, 1998, to Sports Incorporated in Lewiston, Montana (Figure 157).

Figure 157: 3" full lug Target Model 60-13 **CCB4700**, .38 S&W Special. PC 102439.

Figure 158 & inset: Chiefs Special Model 60-9 Lady Smith **CDW4173**, .357 Magnum.

The .357 Magnum Chiefs Special Model 60-9 Lady Smith serial number **CDW4173** bears the model's standard 2⅛" full lug barrel and OEM Altamont smooth laminated rosewood combat stocks sans S&W medallions (Figure 158). S&W shipped it with a trigger lock in a jewel case in February 2000 (inset: top of jewel case). PC 149599.

Here are examples of two quite different Model 36-9 Lady Smiths. Both come in jewel boxes, have blue finishes, and wear OEM Altamont smooth laminated boot stocks. Model 36-9 serial number **CDU4829** has the serial number stamped on the butt and on the frame in the yoke cut, .38 S.&W. SPL stamped on the right of the barrel, and Smith & Wesson stamped on the left. Model 36-9 serial number **CFA5647** has no serial number on the butt, no text stamped on the left side of the barrel, and Smith & Wesson is stamped above .38 S. &W. SPL on the right side of its barrel (either the space between the S. and the ampersand or the lack of a space between the ampersand and the W. appears to be a mistake, and white fill in the text exacerbates the problem.)

- -

Wouldn't I like to find these Chiefs Specials from 1996-2000?

1) 2" Model 36-9 Lady Smith

2) 2" Model 37-3, J-Magnum frame

3) 2⅛" full lug barrel Model 60-9

4) 2" Chiefs Special Model 60-12

5) 3" Heavy Barrel Chiefs Special Model 36-1, two-tone, seventy-five assembled using leftover nickel ADB serial range frames from 1983; blue barrels, cylinders, screws, and thumbpieces; laminated rosewood presentation stocks; assembled and shipped in 1999

- -

S&W used leftover parts to assemble a run of Model 37-2s at some point in 2002 or 2003, but year 2000 became the last full year S&W produced an exposed-hammer revolver without an internal lock, and it is the also the year I retired from the United States Air Force.

In 2001 S&W débuted its 2" carbon steel Chiefs Special Model 36-10 and Chiefs Special Airweight Model 37-4, both in .38 S&W Special, along with two stainless Chiefs Specials: Models 60-14 with a 2⅛" full lug barrel and 60-15 with a 3" full lug barrel, both chambered for the .357 Magnum cartridge.

Through 2024 these and the subsequent stainless steel models had an internal lock accessed with a small hex key through a circular hole in the frame above the thumbpiece. The internal lock and its eyesore hole—claimed by some aficionados and reported by multiple news sources to have been put there to appease a certain person with government ties—proved both conceptually and visually unpopular among many collectors, including me.

- -

Postscript: According to several conflicting online sources the Smith & Wesson company underwent at least a few ownership changes in the first two decades of the new millennium. Since sources do seem to contradict each other, I will not attempt to ferret out which might be closer to the truth. Smith & Wesson Brands Incorporated's 2025 website says it spun off from American Outdoor Brands in 2020. Let's start there.

I will simply report the current company owners and management team appear to be on a course to right the ship.

Smith & Wesson sent its handgun product manager to the Smith & Wesson Collectors Association symposium beginning in 2023. We met him, and I immediately assumed a role as antagonist against the annoying and unnecessary internal lock. I was not alone. He promised to carry our strong message back to company executives.

The next year he attended our symposium in Tulsa, Oklahoma, and I dealt another dose of discontent to him. Again, he told us he would be the messenger.

Wonders will never cease.
—English proverb

The most common way people give up their power
is by thinking they don't have any.
—Alice Walker

Never doubt that a small group of thoughtful, committed citizens
can change the world; indeed, it's the only thing that ever has.
—Margaret Mead

2025

Chiefs Special
 Model 36 Classic
 Back to Basics: No Internal Lock

Right on time for the Chiefs Special's 75th Diamond Anniversary, Smith & Wesson débuted its Model 36-11, a redesigned, small, five-shot .38 S&W Special revolver branded "Model 36 Classic No Internal Lock" in January 2025 at the annual SHOT SHOW in Las Vegas, Nevada.

Although the company does not call its new Model 36-11 the Chiefs Special, its features include a 2" barrel, the original Chiefs Special service type front sight, and a retro contoured thumbpiece reminiscent of postwar I-frame Terrier thumbpiece shown on the advertisements in Chapter 1 (Figures 3 & 8). It wears handsome walnut magna stocks with diamonds around the screw and nut escutcheons, and it sports a smaller, revised Smith & Wesson logo on the frame below the new thumbpiece. Model 36-11 serial number **EET3437** flaunts the popular new features (Figure 159). It shipped to Wind River Outdoor Company in Lander, Wyoming, in spring 2025. PC 14076.

Figure 159: The 2025 Smith & Wesson Model 36-11 **EET3437** has no internal lock.

The new Model 36-11 satisfies this collector who has lamented the internal lock model revolvers since Smith & Wesson introduced them in 2001. The company's leaders have shown us they heard us, and better yet, they've proved they were listening. I'm the happier for it.

I offer a hearty Happy Diamond Jubilee, Chiefs Special!

Thank you, Smith & Wesson.

There's still work to do. As I studied the company's website on August 16, 2025, I discovered its historic portrayal of Smith & Wesson's timeline introduces the Chiefs Special in 1950.[17] To the right of a blue ribbon running down the middle of the timeline at the 1950 point, an image portrays the revolver engineers might have emulated to design two features on the new Model 36-11, the front sight and the thumbpiece.

The text left of the ribbon identifies the new 1950 revolver as "The Model 36, Chief's Special®." The possessive Chief's Special does not portray the trademarked name, and calling it a Model 36 in 1950 is about eight years early.

The real shocker for me was the ®, which announces Smith & Wesson had a registered trademark for the CHIEFS SPECIAL model.

Whoever designed the graphic for Smith & Wesson knew that truth, thank goodness, but it's the first time I had ever seen the trademark symbol associated with Chiefs Special.

By agreement, Smith & Wesson had authorized use of company trademarked names and logos in this book, but the agreement did not include the model names Chiefs Special, Airweight, or Lady Smith. My publisher's quick reaction found the United States Patent and Trademark Office's link to the form showing the CHIEFS SPECIAL trademark registration (Figure 123, Chapter 6). Subsequently we discovered the two trademark registrations for Airweight and Lady Smith. The publisher's note to Smith & Wesson's intellectual property honcho resulted in an amended agreement, which solved a dilemma—we could use the model names in my book with the company's permission.

The whole is more than the sum of its parts.
—Aristotle

Part 2

Bits & Bobs

Thanks for your curiosity.
—David Yamane

Research is formalized curiosity.
It is poking and prying with a purpose.
—Zora Neale Hurston

Chapter 10

Model J and Chiefs Special Thumbpieces

For decades Smith & Wesson had used contoured thumbpieces to release the cylinders on its revolvers. The practice continued on the first Model J and early Chiefs, but the second and third ones to ship and others wore a new flat thumbpiece. Flat thumbpieces evolved through seven variations in the first fifteen years. Then Smith & Wesson reverted back to the contoured thumbpiece, and it reigned for a bit more than three decades before Smith & Wesson replaced it with a beveled thumbpiece. History repeats itself. Another twenty-nine years passed, and in 2025 Smith & Wesson again returned to a contoured thumbpiece.

When I first became interested in Chiefs Specials, consensus on the street suggested Smith & Wesson used the contoured thumbpiece on Chiefs up through serial number 110. Serial number 111 was the first at the time believed to wear a flat thumbpiece. Contemporary wisdom also suggested only three flat thumbpiece variations existed.

Frontal, face-on thumbpiece photos are on the left of each pair; profile photos are on the right. All frontal photos are equal height so profiles show the thumbpieces out of proportion—longer or shorter.

President Hellstorm's serial number **6** was the first Model J to be delivered in October 1950 (Figures 160 & 161). It wears a contoured thumbpiece, which the company used on several known blue and nickel Chiefs into 1951. Chiefs known to wear the thumbpiece span serial range **4** through **117**, but not all Chiefs in the range wear it.

Figures 160 & 161: Contoured thumbpiece from Chiefs Special **72**, 1950/51.

S&W delivered the next two Model Js, serial numbers **X58** and **10**, on December 6, 1950. Both wear the first known flat thumbpiece. Other blue Model Js and Chiefs known to wear the thumbpiece are serial numbers **16**, **32**, **54**, **99**, and **101**. Their ship dates, not in serial order, range from December 1950 through August 1951 (Figures 162 & 163).

The flat thumbpiece has eleven ridges, twelve valleys, a slight back-to-front incline, is rather blockish, and its face-on height is a mere quarter inch. Collectors hadn't identified this thumbpiece when I began my journey. I brought it into public view when I found serial number **99** a few years on. We've since discovered the other Chiefs with this thumbpiece.

Figures 162 & 163: First flat thumbpiece, 1950/51, ¼" tall. Eleven ridges.

The first known second flat thumbpiece débuted on serial number **111** on April 11, 1951. The thumbpiece has an oval shape, and its profile view shows a bit more of a back-to-front incline (Figures 164 & 165). Future flat thumbpieces share its three-eighths-inch height, and like the first flat thumbpiece, it has eleven ridges and twelve valleys. Known Chiefs Special serial numbers with this thumbpiece span serial range **111** to **36722**, and that last one shipped on September 10, 1953.

Figures 164 & 165: Second flat thumbpiece, 1951-1953, ⅜" tall. Eleven ridges.

Due to milling differences the ridges on some flat thumbpieces vary between sharp peaks and somewhat flat, butte-like summits above the valleys. Some may consider each of these as different or distinct flat thumbpieces, but I do not because the variations tend to intermingle, for now making it impossible to pinpoint eras when each exists.

The first known Chiefs Special with the third flat thumbpiece is Chiefs Special Airweight serial number **28799**. Smith & Wesson shipped it in December 1953. This distinct thumbpiece sports ten ridges and eleven valleys and has a slight ramp at the front of its incline (Figures 166 & 167). The last known third flat thumbpiece shipped in March 1955 on Chiefs Special serial number **54832**.

Figures 166 & 167: Third flat thumbpiece, 1953-1955. Ten ridges.

I identified another previously unknown fourth flat thumbpiece when I found nickel Chiefs Special serial number **47475** (Figures 168 & 169). Smith & Wesson gave this Chiefs Special to Sales Manager H. O. Austin on August 30, 1954, and the invoice said he would use it "for demonstration purposes." It is the least frequently seen flat thumbpiece; I have seen and documented four of this style with seven ridges and eight valleys, all with a nickel finish. Other known examples reside on Chiefs Special serial numbers **47488** and **48403** and I-frame 1953 .22/32 Kit Gun serial number 3553. Like the third flat thumbpiece, this one has a raised ramp at the front.

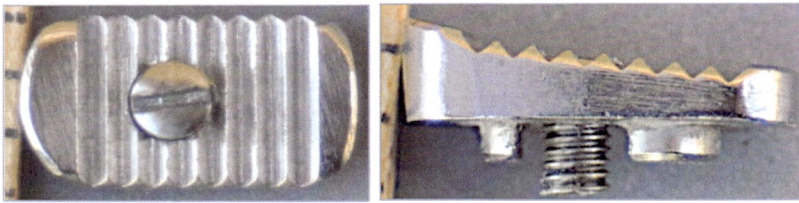

Figures 168 & 169: Fourth flat thumbpiece, nickel only, 1954. Seven ridges.

A fifth flat thumbpiece first appeared on Chiefs Special Airweight **52620** in February 1955. It shows up on both blue and nickel Chiefs, and it reverted back to eleven ridges and twelve valleys with a taller, more angled ramp at the front (Figures 170 & 171). The screw securing it to the bolt spans ridges four through six and just cuts into the left side of the seventh ridge. Milling variations make this thumbpiece tough to distinguish from the sixth flat thumbpiece without seeing the profile.

I suspect the ones I identify as the fifth, sixth, and seventh flat thumbpieces were formerly believed to be the same thumbpiece due to their similarities, especially when seen from the face and not the profile. I estimate Smith & Wesson shipped the last of the fifth flat thumbpieces in early 1957.

Figures 170 & 171: Fifth flat thumbpiece, 1955-1957. Eleven ridges.

The sixth flat thumbpiece also has eleven ridges and twelve valleys. Its screw also spans ridges four through six and cuts into the seventh ridge (variations exist), but the front ramp is steeper and taller. Chiefs Special serial number **93475** was the first I documented with this thumbpiece, and it shipped on January 11, 1957 (Figures 172 & 173). The last one I've noted is on serial number **243089**, and it probably shipped in 1961.

Figures 172 & 173: Sixth flat thumbpiece, 1957-1961. Eleven ridges.

The seventh and last known flat thumbpiece has twelve ridges and thirteen valleys, making it the easiest to distinguish from the two previous styles. I believe this one was also unknown before I identified the twelve ridges and different profile. It's the same height at the sixth style, but it has a less abrupt front ramp. I first noted it on serial number **204783**; it likely shipped in 1961. The last known Chiefs Special with this flat thumbpiece is serial number **445939**. Due to what seems to have been an overnight execution of the engineering change to the next thumbpiece it might have shipped as late as early February 1966 (Figures 174 & 175).

Figures 174 & 175: Seventh flat thumbpiece, 1961-1966. Twelve ridges.

I am unsure, and a bit sketchy, on specific serial numbers when all but the last of this last trio of flat thumbpieces appeared and went away. The lack of detail relates to me not knowing to track the variations until I identified their differences quite some time after I began documenting Chiefs in my database. When I review early data entries, which simply say "flat thumbpiece," I cannot tell which of the last three thumbpieces each Chiefs Special wore near the overlap years, and it's impossible to go back to myriad sources where I got the details to revise the database because auctions, for example, time out in short order.

Smith & Wesson used a contoured thumbpiece identical to early Chiefs thumbpieces when it produced thirty-nine stainless steel Chiefs Special Model 60s in the summer of 1965. The company then issued an engineering change on February 11, 1966, to replace all flat thumbpieces with new contoured thumbpieces. The first known carbon steel Chiefs Special with a contoured thumbpiece is Model 36 serial number **404634**, and it shipped on February 21, 1966 (Figures 176 & 177).

Figures 176 & 177: Contoured thumbpiece, 1966-1996.

Smith & Wesson replaced the contoured thumbpiece with a new beveled thumbpiece in 1996 when it changed from forged parts to new metal injection molded parts for its thumbpieces, hammers, and triggers (Figures 178 & 179). I document serial numbers of the era, and I have begun to analyze the Chiefs Special models' serial numbers around the transition. It seems the change occurred amid the CAL-CAM prefixes.

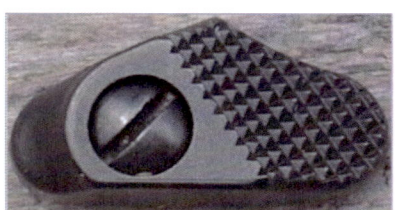 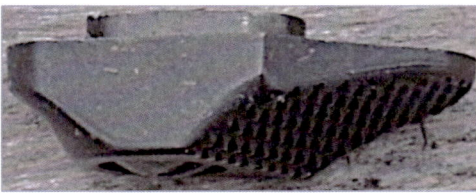

Figures 178 & 179: Beveled thumbpiece, top profile, 1996-2024.

When Smith & Wesson did away with the internal lock on Model 36-11 in early 2025, the company reverted back to a contoured thumbpiece (Figures 180 & 181). No Chiefs Special ever wore one that looked like this new thumbpiece with its hour-glass waist between the nut and the contour where the thumb fits, but it was known on prewar and postwar I-frames into the early 1950s. Early Chiefs Specials wore the full-bodied contoured thumbpiece shown in Figures 160 and 161 on page 148.

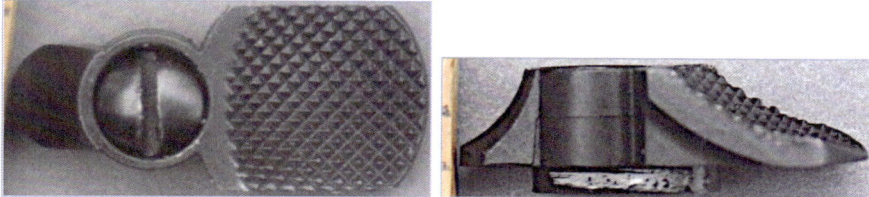

Figures 180 & 181: Contoured thumbpiece, 2025—Diamond Jubilee year.

I by no means intend to suggest or imply here that these are the only thumbpieces Smith & Wesson used on Chiefs Specials in the model's seventy-five years. Having documented less than one percent of Chiefs Special production through these decades, I hold no claim that perhaps there is not at least one more variation on the flat thumbpiece theme. I will continue to be curious, and we'll see. I ask you to please do the same.

The hole in the contoured thumbpiece fits over a threaded part affixed to the bolt, and a nut with a screw driver slot secures the contoured thumbpiece to its bolt (Figure 182). A screw pokes through the hole in a flat thumbpiece and screws into a threaded nut on the bolt (Figure 183). Photos taken with thumbpieces removed so the views of the bolts are limited to the machined openings in the frames where the thumbpieces seat. Swapping flat and contoured thumbpieces also requires changing the bolt, which involves removing the side plate, the mainspring and rod, and then the hammer to gain access to the bolt.

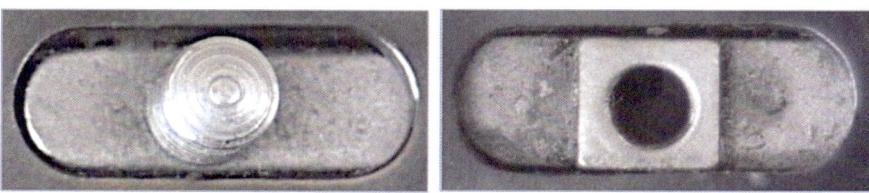

Figure 182: Bolt for contoured thumbpiece. Figure: 183: Bolt for flat thumbpiece.

How little we know of what there is to know.
—Ernest Hemingway

Chapter 11

And, and, and …
Model J and Chiefs Special Ampersands

Smith & Wesson used ampersands in three places on its carbon and stainless steel Chiefs Special revolvers: in the Smith & Wesson text on the left side of the barrel, in the Smith & Wesson text on the four lines of text on the right side of the frame, and in "S&W" in the caliber on the right side of the barrel (Figure 184). Chiefs Special Airweights and Model 37s did not use "S&W" in the caliber on the right side of the barrel.

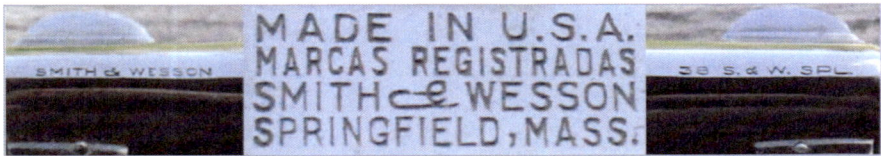

Figure 184: Ampersands on serial number **72**, 1951.

Originally Smith & Wesson used what I identify as the company's traditional ampersand. It has an unusual type style with a bulbous bloom left of center. Each location seemed to have its own unique design, often with ampersands in the third line of text on the frame in the early Chiefs showing the bloom's wildest, almost cartoon-like extreme.

Inconsistency seemed to be the only constant regarding the size and shape of the ampersands through the 1950s. Examples on my 3" Chiefs Special Model 36 shipped in 1959 make my point (Figure 185).

Figure 185: 3" Chiefs Special Model 36 serial number **158956**, 1959.

Beginning in 1963 I noted a transition to more uniform and generic ampersands in all locations on the Chiefs Specials, both Models 36 and 37 and then the Model 60 in 1966. The transition period lasted at least six years before the generic ampersand seemed to become the standard in all three locations, at least on most models with 2" barrels (Figure 186).

Figure 186: Generic Chiefs Special ampersands on serial number **J839971**, 1981.

In 1969 ampersands on the left side of 3" barrel models began to have no rhyme or reason. First a generic ampersand alternated with a new style that resembled an 8 with letter c kerned close: &c (Figure 187).

Figure 187: Chiefs Special Model 36 **J53346**, &c ampersand, 1969-1973.

In 1973, a first on a Model 36-1, we see a stylized variation of the traditional ampersand. It's on one known shipment to a large Smith & Wesson exporter. Few in the shipment appear in the U.S.A. (Figure 188).

Figure 188: 3" Heavy Barrel Model 36-1 **J218723**, traditional ampersand, 1973.

The last oddball ampersand on 3" Chiefs is Greek letter *epsilon* (ε) (Figure 189). We see it on 3" Models 36, 36-1, and 37 for two years: 1975/76, then the generic ampersand came into favor.

Figure 189: 3" Model 36 serial number **J349996**, *epsilon* ampersand, 1975.

Ah, not in knowledge is happiness,
but in the acquisition of knowledge!
—Edgar Allan Poe

Chapter 12

Chiefs Special Stocks

This chapter shows the stocks on Chiefs Specials in my collection and identifies several other known variations. I do not profess that these are the only stocks Smith & Wesson used on its Chiefs through the years. Others I do not own certainly could exist.

Smith & Wesson primarily used walnut to create standard stocks for its revolvers. The earliest Chiefs Specials with five-screw frames wore either checked walnut magna or service stocks with diamonds around flush-mounted screw and nut escutcheons. Smith & Wesson medallions sink flush into the top portion of each stock. The last known service stocks are on Chiefs Special serial number **117**. Some gifts for friends of Smith & Wesson wore smooth magna presentation stocks of either walnut, rosewood, or other woods with S&W medallions (Figure 190). During the Korean War years (1950-1953) the company changed the material for medallions several times depending upon what was available due to wartime needs, even turning to plastic for a time.

Figure 190: *Left* to *right*: Five-screw J-frame service, magna, and presentation stocks.

The advent of the new four-screw J-frame lengthened the grip frame by one-eighth inch and extended the stocks by the same measure (Figure 191). The figure shows the shorter (five-screw) walnut diamond magna and rosewood presentation stocks on the left and the new longer rosewood presentation and walnut diamond magna stocks on the right.

Figure 191: Five-screw magna and presentation; four-screw presentation and magna.

S&W ordered elimination of the diamonds around countersunk escutcheons and escutcheon nuts on January 11, 1966. The change took a few years to implement. Figure 192 shows square butt walnut diamond magna stocks, escutcheon flush with the diamond (*left*) and escutcheon countersunk into new diamond-less stock (*center*). The checking pattern is nearly the same on both, except a straight line replaced the slight smile at the upper border. Late in 1968 or early 1969 Smith & Wesson changed the checking pattern, narrowing it and shortening its height (*right*).

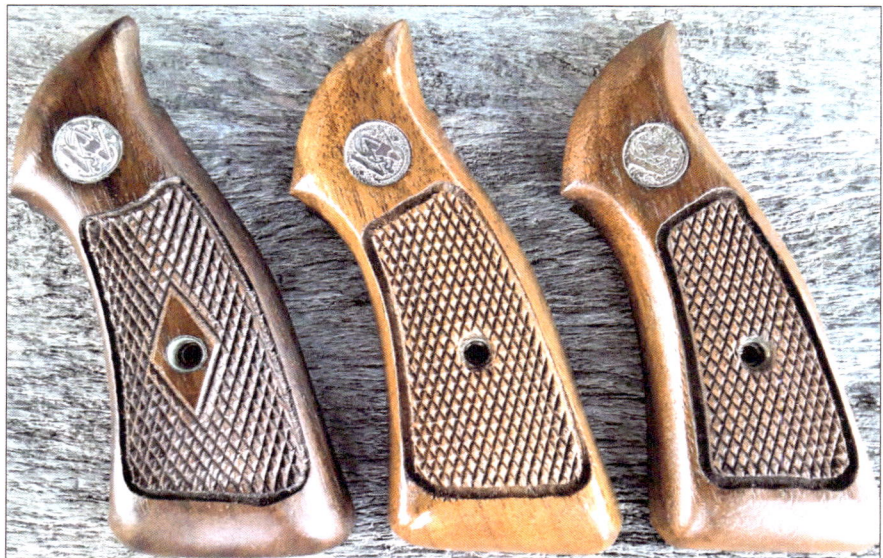

Figure 192: Three checking styles on square butt magna stocks, 1968/69.

Figure 193 shows the same progression from diamond magna to magna to the reduced checking area on round butt magna stocks in the late 1960s. Round butt stocks lost their upper smile in 1968/69, and they also all but lost their lower pout. Through the early '90s the company used this last style with slight variations, including a variety of pouts.

Figure 193: Three checking styles on round butt magna stocks, 1968/69.

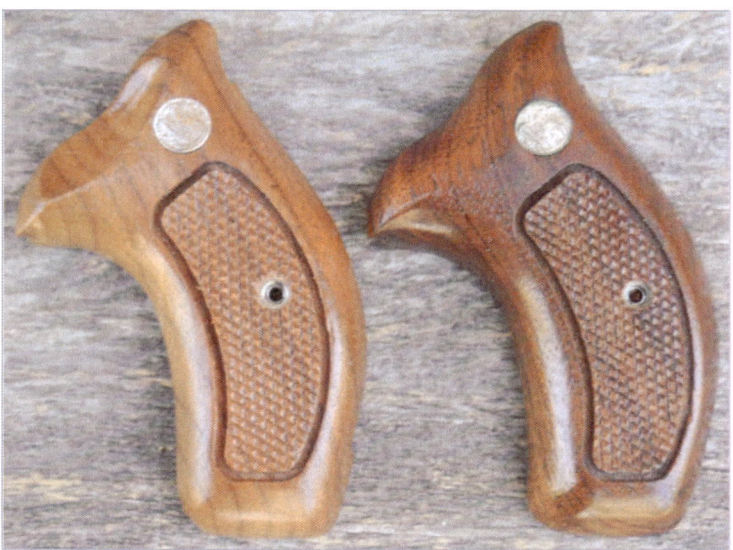

Figure 194: Banana stocks with and without a speed loader cutout.

Through this era we also see wood stocks in what Dr. Jinks calls "banana" style. Figure 194 shows ones from the blue Model 60 and a Model 36-1. The left stock has a speed loader cutout, and the stock on the right has an unusual top treatment that resembles a whale tail. We see others with a full rounded top sans speed loader cutout. We also see smooth banana stocks with and without the speed loader cutout.

Another popular stock during this era, a round-to-square butt target stock, fit either round or square butt frames (shown in Figure 195 on a Model 50). They came checked or smooth, with or without a speed loader cutout.

Figure 195: Round-to-square butt target stocks on Model 50.

Presentation stocks through the Bangor Punta era (1965-1984) showed great variety (Figure 196).

Figure 196: Presentation stocks during Bangor Punta's ownership.

When Smith & Wesson introduced its Chiefs Special Lady Smith models in 1989, it put Goncalo Alves combat style stocks with no pinky finger groove, reportedly designed to fit women's hands, on models with

163

3" barrels. The company put smooth laminated rosewood magna stocks on Lady Smith models with 2" barrels (Figure 197).

Figure 197: Lady Smith 3" Goncalo Alves and 2" laminated rosewood stocks, 1989.

S&W's Goncalo Alves combat stocks with a pinky finger groove shipped on some models, and they were available aftermarket at gun shops. They're shown here on a 1989 double action only Model 36-2 (Figure 198).

Figure 198: S&W Combat Stocks on a 1989 DAO Model 36-2, 1989.

Beginning in 1989 Smith & Wesson began to experiment using various rubber grips and wood stocks made by different manufacturers. Hogue was one of the companies to make rubber original equipment manufacturer (OEM) grips, and Smith & Wesson put its Monogrip on a special run of 2,000 3" Chiefs Special Target Model 36-6s that year (Figure 199). S&W also used Hogue's Bantam grips on a limited run of 2" Chiefs Special Model 36-2s, which feature a factory bobbed hammer and came in a double action only configuration (Figure 200).

Figure 199: Hogue Monogrip on Chiefs Special Target Model 36-6, 1989.

Figure 200: Hogue Bantam boot grip on Chiefs Special Model 36-2 DAO, 1989.

During the 1990s Smith & Wesson used Uncle Mike's boot and combat stocks modeled in rubber after renowned stock maker Craig Spegel's wood stock designs (Figures 201 & 202).

Figure 201: Uncle Mike's boot grips on Model 36-8, 1994.

Figure 202: Uncle Mike's combat grips on Model 60-11, 1998.

Smith & Wesson began to use Altamont's laminated rosewood boot and combat stocks without S&W medallions on its new J-Magnum frame Lady Smith models in 1996. Figure 203 shows the combat style on a Model 60-9 from 2000.

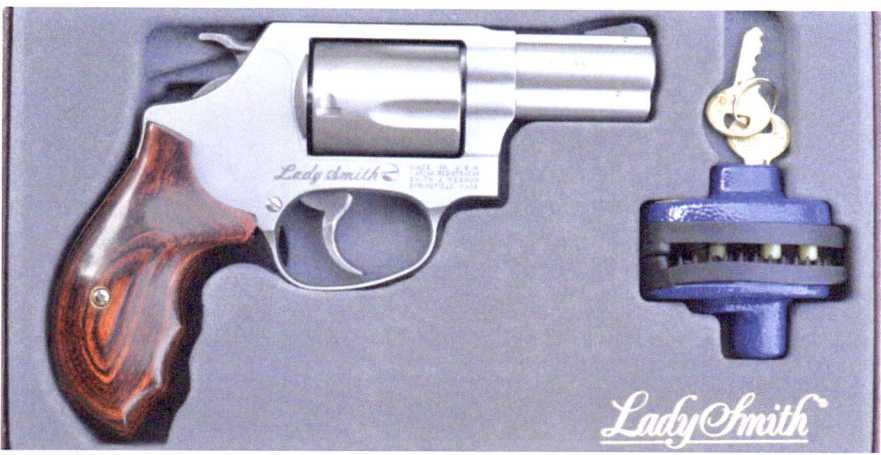

Figure 203: Altamont laminated rosewood combat stocks on Lady Smith Model 60-9.

Smith & Wesson introduced its No Internal Lock Model 36-11 in January 2025, and its stocks are walnut diamond magnas (Figure 204).

Figure 204: Walnut diamond magna stocks for a Model 36-11, 2025.

To a child, often the box a toy came in
is more appealing than the toy itself.
—Allen Klein

Chapter 13

Chiefs Special Boxes

Smith & Wesson used a plain red box to house its first Chiefs Specials. Based on seeing the earliest known models in their original, serial numbered boxes, they didn't even have a label on the end to tell us what was inside. Through the '50s and into the early '60s serial numbers are handwritten in grease pencil on one end of the bottom of the box.

When I began collecting Chiefs I wasn't the least bit interested in boxes, especially if the serial number on the box didn't match the gun inside. I focused on models based on their attributes and whether they fit into my plan for them to help tell the Chiefs' story. Perhaps covert peer pressure or some other influence took hold, and once I began to gather a fair number of examples in better condition, and also in their original boxes, I began to better appreciate the containers and changed my thinking a wee bit. I don't have representatives of every style of box the company used through the '50s and '60s, but in addition to showing a few of mine I'll describe details of several variations Smith & Wesson Collectors Association friend Francis Zandome has shared with me. He goes all out to track down and document box details.

My oldest Chiefs Special (based on its ship date) is also the one with my lowest serial number. Smith & Wesson shipped serial number **72** as a gift to Flora Van Orden on March 7, 1951. It came in this red box, and it does not have a label on either end of the box (Figure 205).

Figure 205: Red box for Flora (Mitchell) Van Orden's Chiefs Special serial number **72**.

My next boxed Chiefs Special was also a gift to Flora Van Orden. It's an early Chiefs Special Airweight (Figure 206). I can't explain why its metal corners are shorter than ones on other boxes. Figure 207 shows the somewhat worn grease pencil serial number on the bottom of the box.

Figure 206: Label on Flora Van Orden's Chiefs Special Airweight serial number **24298**.

Figure 207: Grease pencil serial number **24298** on the bottom of the box.

The label on a later Chiefs Special Airweight's original box shows a slight modification (Figure 208).

Figure 208: Ink Airweight stamps on the label of serial number **27621**.

Although the serial number on the bottom of this box doesn't match the gun, my second 3" Chiefs Special came in a red box with the correct label (Figure 209). The gun shipped in May 1954, and I believe this box with its original gun did, too.

Figure 209: Red box with a label for a 3" Chiefs Special, 1954.

I don't have a box for any of my Chiefs from 1955 through 1958, but my January 1955-shipped S&W Centennial came in its original box, and the top is identical to the boxes used for Chiefs beginning that year (Figure 210). Some collectors have named the box SunRay or SunBurst due to their perception of "rays" extending from the S&W logo (the sun) at the top left, which illuminate the diagonal text at the bottom right.

Figure 210: Smith & Wesson Centennial box top, shipped in January 1955.

Another variation of the ray box from 1959 shows the text at the bottom right side of the box parallel with the bottom edge of the box (Figure 211). Francis Zandome sent a photo of a box from this era for a nickel gun. It is the same as a blue gun's box, except the label on the end has red text. That's why you see both finish colors identified on the creative label of the box containing my two-tone Chiefs Special (Figure 212). Again, note the incorrect model name. Also note a variation in the box's border compared to the 1955 Centennial box. Other blue boxes Francis shared with me had no border or graphics on the top, and others showed several different border designs.

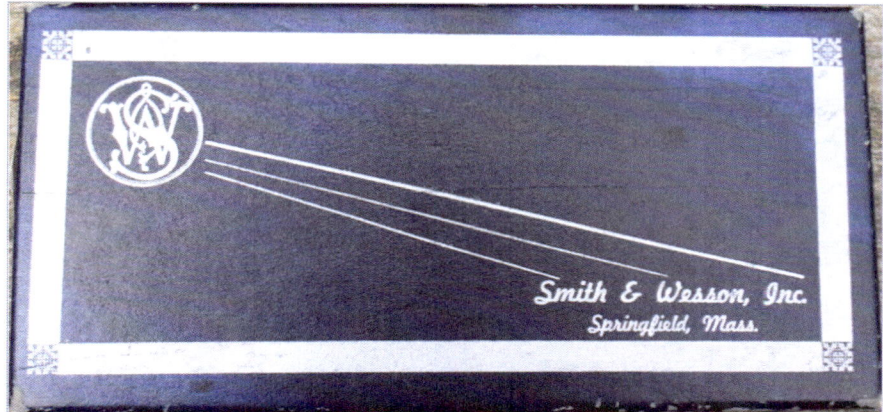

Figure 211: Chiefs Special box top for two-tone Model 36 serial number **158956**.

Figure 212: Box end label for two-tone Chiefs Special serial number **158956**.

At some point in the early 1960s Smith & Wesson deleted the sunrays and moved the company name back to the diagonal at the lower right of the box with outlines above and below the name (Figure 213). The new boxes also included a stamped end with details of the model inside the box and its specifics. A grease pencil serial number continued to appear on the bottom. Beyond about '61 the other end of the boxes gained a preprinted label with the blanks filled in by an inspector and a packer, and the grease pencil serial number on the bottom went away (Figure 214). Usually inspector's and packer's ink colors are different.

Figure 213: 1960s Chiefs Special box with angled text and outlines above and below.

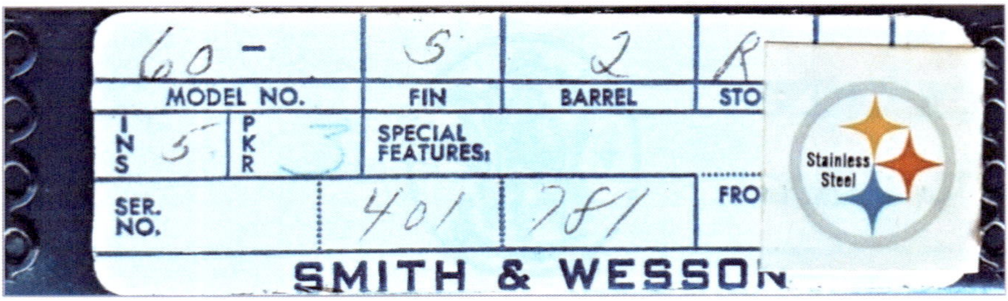

Figure 214: Box end label for a Model 60 shipped in October 1965.

Stainless steel Chiefs Specials used the same blue boxes as carbon steel and Airweight models with a blue finish. (Figure 215).

Figure 215: Stamped box end for a stainless steel Chiefs Special Model 60.

The company changed the box color for nickel Chiefs Specials in this era; they were gray, although I've seen nickel Chiefs in blue boxes with stamped and handwritten labels identifying the contents as nickel.

After Bangor Punta bought Smith & Wesson in late 1965 we see the Bangor Punta name and brand appear on the boxes as you see it in Figure 216.

Figure 216: Bangor Punta name and brand on box top, 1966-1968.

By the late 1960s the Bangor Punta brand and name changed on the boxes, and we see this version until Bangor Punta sold the company to Lear Siegler in January 1984 (Figure 217).

Figure 217: Revised Bangor Punta brand and name, 1969-1983.

Figure 218: Somebody ignored history and made the Chiefs name possessive on the box.

Despite S&W applying for Chiefs Special trademark protection in April 1974, near that time somebody thought the Chiefs name should be possessive on the box ends (Figure 218). I'll spare you my dissertation on the "Cool Hand Luke" syndrome and its results when "What we," an organization's internal entities, "have here is a failure to communicate."

As early as 1981 we begin to see the new one-piece boxes with computer-generated labels (Figure 219). We continue to see some early one-piece boxes, though, with older handwritten labels.

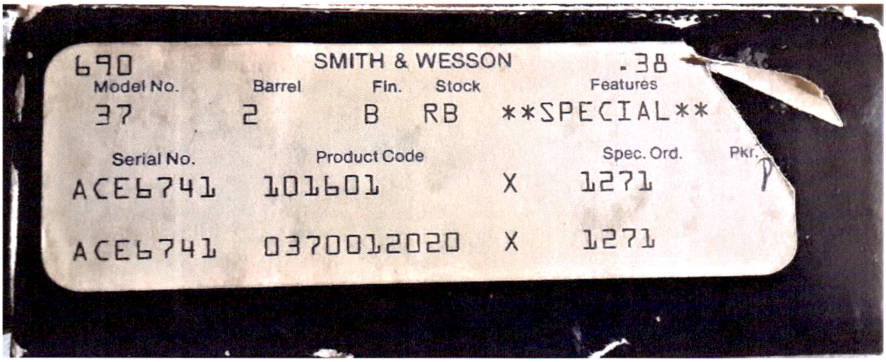

Figure 219: Computer-generated label on the new one-piece box, 1981.

Figure 220: One-piece boxes with progressive labeling shown on the lower right side of the front as Smith & Wesson changed hands in the 1980s.

Figure 220 shows a stack of the one-piece boxes as the company evolved through three owners. Bangor Punta's logo is on the bottom box, Lear Siegler added its logo on the short front of the box after it bought the company in 1984 (middle box), and the top box shows how R. L. Tompkins only used the company's original logo and name on the boxes after it acquired the company in 1987. Tompkins also added a Made in The USA sticker with an eagle on the front left of its boxes.

You saw the variety of containers Lady Smiths came in from the late '80s through 2000 in Chapters 7 and 8. Those shipped in cardboard boxes of various sizes and shapes to accommodate the containers. Some, but few, Lady Smith models came in the one-piece boxes with no fancy container and identified in the Features heading on computer-generated labels as Lady Smith.

Original, early Performance Center offerings (not for the Chiefs Specials) came in an aluminum briefcase style, hinged container with two metal clasps on the front. When the Performance Center created a special model based on the Chiefs Special Model 60, they came in blue plastic hinged boxes with two clasps and a Performance Center logo embossed on the box top. A paper label was affixed to the end, but all too often the label does not remain attached.

With the advent of the J-Magnum frame the cardboard box lost its hold and gave way to a large plastic hinged blue box with two plastic clasps.

The large boxes gave way to a smaller, more appropriately sized blue plastic hinged box with two smaller clasps.

The 2025 box for the new Model 36-11 seems to have grown up again to about the same size as the mid-'90s blue plastic boxes.

The greatest thing about ideas
is being able to share them.
—Albert Einstein

I didn't build my Chiefs Special collection with a goal of having "as new" examples through the spectrum. The "warts and all" on a few show through the camera's lens. I wanted my herd of Chiefs Specials to tell the model's story. The herd is not yet complete, and it may never be because the ones I need to complete the story may never come into view. I believe my current herd, a few special others I've discovered along this path, and my research about ones I'm missing allowed me to adequately narrate the story.

I consider twelve models as the "cornerstones" of my collection's dodecagonal foundation. Here are those cornerstones, their ship dates, and why I see each as a foundational piece of my Chiefs Special collection:

- Chiefs Special **72**, March 7, 1951
  - • My first carbon steel five-screw, for Flora Van Orden
- Chiefs Special Airweight **24298**, February 11, 1953
  - • My first alloy four-screw, for Flora Van Orden
- Chiefs Special 3" **30375**, July 17, 1953
  - • My first 3" carbon steel five-screw
- Chiefs Special Nickel **47475**, August 30, 1954
  - • My first carbon steel four-screw, for Harold Austin
- Chiefs Special Airweight **60625**, April 1, 1955
  - • My first alloy three-screw
- Chiefs Special **93475**, January 11, 1957
  - • My first carbon steel three-screw
- Chiefs Special Model 36 **126017**, September 4, 1958
  - • First known carbon steel Model 36
- Chiefs Special Model 60 **401781**, October 21, 1965
  - • My first stainless Model 60
- Chiefs Special Model 60 **410056**, July 12, 1972
  - • Only known (in the U.S.A.) blued stainless Model 60
- Chiefs Special Model 36-1 **458157**, July 28, 1967
  - • My first Model 36-1
- Chiefs Special Target Model 50 **935J93**, March 27, 1973
  - • My first Model 50
- Chiefs Special Model 60-1 **R57195**, June 12, 1978
  - • My first stainless 3" Model 60 with a square butt

Membership in the Smith & Wesson Collectors Association has proven most rewarding. Members number far more than 1,000, and akin to too many organizations, the truly active, engaged members count about ten percent of the community. The engaged members, though, do count as the most knowledgeable folks I've met regarding the history of Smith & Wesson. Interactively the group is akin to having access to a living encyclopedia of the company, its rich history, and all its products from 1852 through today. My greatest concern is the average age of our active members. We must attract young folks to engage in the science and art of Smith & Wesson, past and present, and carry our torch into the 'morrow.

To join the Smith & Wesson Collectors Association hop online, and go to https://forum.theswca.org/. Click the "Welcome" link, then click "Join Us!" and then the link to the membership application. Mail the completed application and your membership fee to the address near the bottom of the form. Our administrator will contact you post haste.

The three key features of membership are the Smith & Wesson Collectors Association's *Journal*, a three-time-a-year, full-color publication featuring member's articles on all things Smith & Wesson; access to the organization's website and its contents, which includes forums to engage with other knowledgeable members, digital copies of past *Journal*s, and other terrific resources; databases on a variety of specific models curated by Association members, which includes my Chiefs Special database; and a grand opportunity to attend the organization's annual symposium, where members gather to show off their best examples and collections of Smith & Wesson models and share the best, most detailed, and in-depth information available anywhere in the world.

The Association offers members and non-members, both, the opportunity to obtain an official historical letter for any Smith & Wesson model in existence. Membership enables you to get a reduced price for the cost of a letter. Mind you there are a scant few examples for which no details or other information can be found.

You might have an interest in supporting the Smith & Wesson Historical Foundation, the Association's extended arm for research. The Foundation has so far digitized the records for Smith & Wesson models through about 1967. After obtaining an official historic letter on your model, you may ask the Foundation for a "deep dive" into the archived records to obtain other documents associated with the serial number, which might include a copy of the original factory invoice and any other correspondence related to your gun. Some documents are fascinating.

The *Smith & Wesson Forum*, owned by Smith & Wesson Collectors Association member Lee Jarrett, is an outstanding gathering place and resource for collectors and others interested in S&W models. I identify it as the primary conduit for S&W aficionados to transition into Smith & Wesson Collectors Association membership, as I did quite a few years ago. While it is possible to be a forum member without any cost, you may choose to become a supporting member by donating an annual contribution to obtain full-screen access, along with other benefits.

Folks frequently ask me three questions. "How long have you been collecting Chiefs Specials?" "Where did you find all your Chiefs?" "How did you accumulate all the knowledge you have about the various Chiefs Special models?" Many find it surprising that I first became interested in Chiefs Specials about ten years ago. I've been buying Smith & Wesson revolvers for more than five decades so I have a reasonable, basic grasp of the company and all its models, and I've owned and shot everything from I-frames in .22 long rifle and .32 Long to long-barreled and snub-nosed 500 Magnums, but other than a brand-new Model 60 I owned in the early '80s I bought my first Chiefs Special in 2015. That one spurred my call to arms!

As I studied the model and its history I became emersed in the details and wanted to know more … and more … and more. The result after a decade became adding Chiefs from shows within the state, online sellers and auctions, and friends within the Smith & Wesson Collectors Association. The collection shown herein, Dr. Jinks' wonderful support, help and contributions of myriad other friends, and a decade of in-depth analysis allowed me to compile and narrate the story you see here.

I offer my typical word of caution about research: Be wary about believing the first thing you discover as you search for information about a Smith & Wesson model in your viewfinder, whether you inherited it from a family member, bought it from a friend, or found it another way. The world is full of braggarts who believe they know it all. You know them; many use the text-speak "IMHO" in nearly every communication. The *Latin* term *caveat emptor*, "let the buyer beware," applies whether you are only seeking information or buying a model from a local gun shop, a private seller, or another source. Even reputable publications get things a bit off, and as I've experienced—history changes. Be a wee bit skeptical, do your due diligence, and seek out details from knowledgeable folks who will help inform you. Most of us have two eyes and two ears but only one mouth—we should use our allotted assets proportionally.

Above all—no matter your status: beginner or novice, aficionado, accumulator, collector, or all-out specialist—enjoy your journey as you learn about whichever Smith & Wesson models interest you.

Although I borrowed only one quote from David Yamane's book, *Gun Curious, A Liberal Professor's Surprising Journey Inside America's Gun Culture* (my page 6), I included David's book in the bibliography. In June 2025 Dr. Yamane told his story at the Smith & Wesson Collector's Association symposium in Concord, North Carolina. He shared his life experiences and how they resulted in him becoming a gun owner and writing his book. On page 145 I also shared the inscription David wrote in my copy of his book. David's work should be a mandatory read for every voting American and most especially everyone running for office as a lawmaker in our Great Republic.

You've probably noticed I have not delved into the netherworld of "what's it worth?" I am one who believes putting anything in print about gun values is a waste of time and ink. The market ebbs and flows. A document printed today will be out of touch with reality by the time you get it into your hands. Besides, I sought out many oddballs, and their values in no way reflect the majority of plain-Jane models loved by the many who simply want a few representative examples of the marque.

Go to gun shows. Search Internet sales and auction sites. Watch with one blind eye. Listen with one deaf ear. Follow the market for the models you find interesting, and you'll pick up clues as to what folks are generally willing to pay. You will encounter an occasional extreme—high or low. Don't fall into the trap of thinking the extremes are norms. They are not. Along with your experiences you'll come to recognize those wide abnormalities. Your patience and knowledge will serve you well, and by all means figure out what you want based on your budget, your comfort level, your interests, and the condition of the models you find interesting. Have fun!

The end

1. International Association of Chiefs of Police, Resources, *Police Chief* Magazine, accessed December 18, 2024, https://www.policechiefmagazine.org.
2. Lyman and Merrie Wood Museum of Springfield History, Springfield, Massachusetts, accessed August 8, 2025, https://springfieldmuseums.org/about/museum-of-springfield-history/.
3. Springfield Armory National Historic Site, accessed July 8, 2025, https://www.nps.gov/spar/index.htm.
4. "DRAGNET Full Cast and Crew," Internet Movie Database, accessed January 6, 2023, https://www.imdb.com/title/tt0043194/fullcredits/?ref_=ttep_sa_2.
5. "Custom Handgun Grip ID and Collector Guide 1935-2000," Anthony Lombardo, accessed January 10, 2023, https://www.coltforum.com/attachments/joe-blackford-info-by-Lombardo-pdf876613.
6. "LAPD Badges: To Collect and Preserve," *Los Angeles Times*, September 24, 1997, accessed January 13, 2023, https://www.latimes.com/archives/la-xpm-1997-Sep-24-Is-35467-story.html.
7. "In Memory of Lieutenant Daniel N. Cooke," Los Angeles Police Department Online, May 5, 1999, accessed January 28, 2023, https://www.lapdonline.org/newsroom/in-memory-of-lieutenant-daniel-n-cooke/.
8. "Dragnet," Turner Classic Movies, accessed January 12, 2023, https://www.tcm.com/tcmdb/title/73581/dragnet#overview.
9. Los Angeles Police Museum, accessed January 24, 2024, https:www.laphs.org/.
10. "High Quality Laminated Hardwood & Specialty Plywood," Rutland Plywood, accessed 16, 2025, https://www.rutlandplywood.com/.
11. "History of the Steelmark," American Iron and Steel Institute, accessed August 24, 2024, https://www.steel.org/about-aisi/history/history-of-the-steelmark/.
12. Obituary: "Joseph M. Wanenmacher, Jr. of Tulsa, Oklahoma," Stanleys Funeral and Cremation Services, accessed October 29, 2022, https://www.stanleysfuneralhome.com/obituary/joseph-wanenmacher-jr.
13. "History, Significant Dates, 1889-1987 (1959-1961 motto translation)," New South Wales Police Force, accessed December 18, 2024, https://www.police.nsw.gov.au/about_us/history.
14. New South Wales Police Force Badge, Wikipedia, accessed December 18, 2024, https://en.wikipedia.org/wiki/New_South_Wales_Police_Force.
15. ".38 CALIBRE SMITH & WESSON REVOLVER (5 shot) for policewomen 1970s," New South Wales Justice and Police Museum, accessed April 11, 2023, https://mhnsw.au/tags/justice-and-police-museum/. No longer found.
16. Trademark Principal Register, CHIEFS SPECIAL, Registered February 24, 1976, United States Patent and Trademark Office, accessed August 18, 2025, https://tsdr.uspto.gov/documentviewer?caseId=sn73018426&docId=ORC200 51121190619&linkId=19#docIndex=18&page=1.
17. "170 Years of American Stories," accessed August 16, 2025, https://www.smith-wesson.com/ourstory.

Jinks, Roy G., *History of Smith & Wesson*, 8th Printing, North Hollywood, Beinfeld Publishing Incorporated, 1983.

———. "Notes on Early .38 Chiefs Special Shipments." Smith & Wesson Collectors Association *Journal* 39, no. 3 (Fall 2005): 51-54.

Supica, Jim, and Nahas, Richard, *Standard Catalog of Smith & Wesson, 5th Edition*, Appleton, Gun Digest Media, 2024.

Wallack, Louis Robert, *American Pistol & Revolver Design and Performance*, New York, Winchester Press, 1978.

Yamane, David, *Gun Curious, A Liberal Professor's Surprising Journey Inside America's Gun Culture*, Jefferson, Exposit, 2024.

That fellow *Can't* couldn't do anything.
Don't be like him. You can!
—Julia Porter Dymond, Mamo

Bob Townsend (Courtesy of Barbara Townsend)

Born and reared in tiny Wyoming towns. Mamo, Mom's Mom, taught me at age seven to shoot her snub-nosed Smith & Wesson .32 Regulation Police Model 31 revolver. I graduated from high school by the skin of my teeth, warmed the seats in the local community college's classrooms for a year, then draft number 007 rescued me from academia.

After joining the United States Air Force in 1972, I graduated from spy school and worked as a communications analyst at National Security Agency (not because I was smart; I got a top secret clearance because I'd been a clean-cut kid who had held jobs and played a sax in the band). After 'nam I retrained into air traffic control—a job I loved. I told the free world's fighter pilots where to go at the Air Force's busiest desert southwest and overseas airfields. Along this path I went back to school, Embry-Riddle Aeronautical University, to earn bachelor's (1985) and master's (1991) degrees, published a trailblazing pilot-controller communications article in the civilian Air Traffic Control Association's *Journal of Air Traffic Control*, attained the top non-commissioned rank: Chief Master Sergeant, and after 14 assignments in 28 years, I retired.

Research impels me, and I like to write. I went to the University of Wyoming, and after five and a half years I earned a bachelor of arts in journalism with a minor in English. In my last year I edited UW's literary and arts magazine, *Owen Wister Review*. The Associated Collegiate Press named it one of the nation's top ten student magazines of 2005.

I moved to a mountain town with thirty year-round residents, thirty miles from gas and groceries, co-owned a historic inn, hosted 1,400 guests from six continents, offered Wyoming's best selection of single malt Scotch whisky in my Two-bit Cowboy Saloon, and retired again after a decade. Since, I have dedicated myself to historic research, writing, and editing. As a member of the town's historical society board of directors I proposed an anthology to celebrate the tiny town's 150th birthday. I solicited, then edited 104 stories by 52 contributors, including an introduction by Senator Al Simpson. Wyoming Historical Society named it their 2018 book of the year. I've served on boards for the Lander Chamber of Commerce, Wyoming Historical Society annual awards, and Fremont County solid waste disposal district. I am assistant editor of the Smith & Wesson Collectors Association *Journal*.

Still haven't decided what I want to be *if* I grow up. I do know my introduction to a small Smith & Wesson revolver as a boy has much to do with my passion for Chiefs Specials. Thank you, Mamo.

www.ingramcontent.com/pod-product-compliance
Lightning Source LLC
Chambersburg PA
CBRC090836120626
46551CB00007B/673